In Memory Of

My Father-In-Law

Lieutenant Colonel Byrl Gowin, U.S. Army

Served with Patton's Army in Europe during World War II.

My Uncle

Birk Shirah, U.S. Navy

Served on the Aircraft Carrier U.S.S. Wasp in the Pacific during World War II.   When the Wasp was torpedoed by the Japanese Submarine "I-19" on September 15, 1942, in the Coral Sea, Uncle Birk survived after he and his fellow shipmates had to abandon their sinking ship.

In Honor Of

My Sons

Jamie Kitson and Lieutenant Colonel Jake Kitson, U.S. Army

One of my "Number Three Sons"

Major Matthew Ross, U.S.M.C.

My Grandchildren and all my Family

To all those that have served and are serving in our U.S. Armed Services, including their families.

"Jimmy, The Marine"

Preface

On the back of my closet door, I have attached two posters to remind me who I am and what I need to remember as my day progresses. One of the posters simply states "Marines" and the other is a phrase: "Semper Fi," reminding me to always be faithful. I look at them every day when I walk into my closet. They remind me to watch my posture and to conduct myself in a manner that would make God, my family and my country proud of my behavior. They remind me of those that did not make it back home to experience what I have been blessed to experience. I want them and their families to know that I remember their sacrifices. I stop for a moment to say a prayer to honor them and their families. I ask God to place "his full armor" around those individuals currently "in harm's way" and ask him to watch over and comfort their families. I do this because I will not forget the sacrifices made and the sacrifices being made today. The Bible tells us that there is no greater love than for one to lay down their life for their fellow man. I survived combat in Vietnam and did not have to pay the ultimate sacrifice. I give all the credit for that to God. Thank you, Lord!

Over the years, I have written a few things about my Vietnam experience. Some of my poems and brief accounts were attempts on my part to share my thoughts with my family, friends and to honor specific requests. My family and many others have asked me about my Vietnam experience as a Marine. I have told all of them a piece of this or that, but nothing comprehensive. My son, Jake, was probably the most persistent in pushing me to write something comprehensive about my Marine experience in general and my Vietnam experience in particular. In order for me to talk about Vietnam, I must talk about my entire experience as a Marine and how it has affected me throughout my life. They are inseparable. I would not be the person I am today without the training the Marines put me through and the fire of Vietnam that tempered my soul. I truly think my life has more meaning and a deeper richness because of what the Lord has allowed me to witness, both good and bad. Yes, I saw some terrible things in Vietnam and they could have defined my life negatively, but then the Lord, working in His mysterious ways, placed my wife (Kathy) in my life, following that up with allowing me to witness my two sons come into this world through the miracle of birth. I have reveled in my son's achievements and watched them grow into the men they are today. Just when you think you cannot be blessed even more, the Lord blessed me with a wonderful daughter-in-law, five beautiful grandchildren, great family gatherings, terrific friends, an amazing career, a peaceful retirement and time to travel about admiring God's creations. It just does not get much better under Heaven than how the Lord has blessed me and my family. If you do not get anything else out of reading "Jimmy, The Marine," please know that if you are weary and burdened, the Lord's yoke is easy. Go to the Lord with your petitions and your burdens. Trust in the Lord and receive His blessings!

Jim Kitson

"Come to me all you who are weary and burdened, and I will give you rest. Take my yoke upon you and learn from me, for I am gentle and humble in heart, and you will find rest for your souls. For my yoke is easy and my burden is light."

Matthew 11:28-30

"For I know the plans I have for you," declares the Lord, "plans to prosper you and not harm you, plans to give you hope and a future."

Jeremiah 29:11

Table of Contents

"At moments, time seems to stand still in the "Oz" like world of Combat"

"Jimmy, The Marine"

I saw the dark bodies of the rocket propelled grenades (RPGs) as they flashed out of the tree line heading towards the tank we were riding "shotgun" on.   Several of us were firing at movement and muzzle flashes in the tree line as one of the RPG's hit the tank.   I was blown through the air about twenty feet away from the tank and towards the tree line.   The explosion or the sudden impact with the ground knocked me unconscious.   Fortunately, I was able to hang onto my rifle, because when I regained consciousness, a Viet Cong soldier was laying on my legs.   I immediately aimed my rifle at him and shot him several times.   One of my buddies was yelling: "He is dead Kit, watch out in front of you."   As I started firing at movement and muzzle flashes in the tree line, I thought: "That other RPG missed the tank."   "I wonder where it went?"   Now why I would think those thoughts in the middle of a firefight, I do not know.   I guess I must have seen it passing by me while I was in the air after I was blown off the tank or I was going crazy.   Go figure! About the time I got my mind back on what I was supposed to be doing, I noticed two grenades flying through the air directly at me.   I made myself as small as I could as they landed next to me.   When they exploded, I thought I was going to die.   Fortunately for me, I had landed between two furrows of some Vietnamese farmer's garden and the soil absorbed the majority of the blasts.   Not long after the grenade explosions, most of the firing around me stopped and I had a chance to survey the damage to my body.   My right shoulder really hurt and felt dislocated.   I had blood oozing out of several shrapnel wounds to different parts of my body.   My camouflaged helmet cover was partially in my face and there was half of an old-fashioned ice tong hooked in my flak jacket.   It looked to me like the Viet Cong soldier laying on my legs was about to drag me into the Viet Cong positions within the tree line.   A cold chill went throughout my body as I realized that I had nearly been the main attraction at the torture games the Viet Cong had probably planned for their activity that night!   My reverie was interrupted when one of my buddies said that I looked like a limp rag doll flying through the air after the RPG hit the tank.   He said that he did not think I was alive when I hit the ground and could not believe that I could hold onto my rifle.   I looked incredulously at him as I asked him to help me up and point me towards the nearest med-evac chopper.

Jimmy, The Marine

Boot Camp - 1967

Present - 2018

1

A Childhood Wish

Have you ever heard the phrase: "Watch out for what you wish for in life?" This is the story of one of my watch out for what you wish for moments. My story evolves around my childhood wish to be a United States Marine. When I was a child and our chores were finished, we had unencumbered time to devote to our fantasies, at least until my mom called us in for supper, baths and bed. We would spend hours making pretend weapons, from bow and arrows to spears, rifles and a myriad assortment of weapons to fight our battles. We did battle with all types of make-believe enemies. Sometimes we would be the bad guys and sometimes the good guys, always adhering to a strict honor system that would occasionally end in real fights when we thought one or the other of us had cheated about who was killed, wounded or just was not playing right. Most of the time we would just have fun and wonder what a real battle would be like. Fortunately, no one knows what will happen to us in the future and believe me, none of my childhood war games with pretend adversaries resembled any of my experiences in the Marines, especially Vietnam.

I was born in Houston, Texas. My dad was an alcoholic. He was abusive, both mentally and physically. His alcoholism affected his ability to work causing us to move from Texas to Louisiana when I was five years old. When I was eight years old, mom decided to leave my dad because of his carousing around and abusiveness. Sadly, she realized that the destructive nature of alcoholism was at work within him and knew we needed to get away from him. Mom took my youngest sister, my brother and me to Alabama to live with my granddad. Over the years, dad and mom tried to get back together, but it just did not work out for them. Mom was a kind person with a great faith in God. I thank the Lord regularly for her and all the people in my life that took the time to teach, guide and show their love for me.

During the summer before I started my tenth-grade year of high school, my mom and dad got back together and tried to salvage their marriage. We moved from Simmsville, Alabama to Chicago, Illinois. I was not too happy about the move, but thanks to a great mentor and gym teacher at my high school in Chicago, my attitude improved. I started getting in pretty good shape and my study habits improved. Unfortunately, dad's alcoholism caused problems again and mom decided it was time for us to go back to Alabama. We moved back to Simmsville, Alabama during the last part of my tenth-grade year. Fortunately, I maintained a good exercise regimen throughout high school, due to the mentorship of my Chicago high school gym teacher. I wish I could say the same for my study habits. During my senior year, a United States Marine Corps (USMC) recruiter visited my high school. He really painted a picture of what I felt was one of the most honorable endeavors imaginable and I wanted to enlist as soon as possible. My mom told me that she would sign the enlistment papers if I graduated from high school. I graduated and she signed the enlistment paperwork.

Graduating high school was a feat in and of itself. Believe me, I was not a stellar student. I never devoted one hundred per cent of my efforts to studying while in high school, basically doing just enough to graduate. Unbeknownst to me, a wicked curve ball had been thrown at my work ethic and attitude when I signed my USMC enlistment papers. I would soon learn that anything less than one hundred per cent was not acceptable and that to succeed and accomplish your dreams, you had better be prepared to do what it takes. The Marine recruiter advised me to prepare myself for the rigors of boot camp. I pushed myself to do more exercises and ran about 3 miles a day, sometimes twice a day. Thanks to my faith in the Lord and the love of my family, my mental attitude was good. I was about as prepared as I could get when I got on that bus to Parris Island, South Carolina...I thought! I remember the Marine recruiter advising me to not get noticed. He said: "Stay under the radar, son." I was bound and determined to follow that sage advice. It is amazing how our decisions affect our lives. At that time, I did not realize how my Marine training and experiences would help me weather many "storms" throughout my life...in and out of the Marines.

2

The Quest For The Globe and Anchor

The USMC provided a Greyhound bus ticket to Montgomery, Alabama for my pre-enlistment physical. I passed the physical and was sworn into the United States Marine Corps on July 6, 1967. All newly sworn in Marines were given Greyhound bus tickets from Montgomery, Alabama to Parris Island, South Carolina. We arrived at the Parris Island Recruit Depot very late at night (after 12:00 AM) and all of us were excited about what would happen next. In a flurry of noise and shouting, drill instructors swarmed onto our bus. I controlled my comportment pretty good, even while the drill instructors were shouting things concerning our lineage and asking us why we were still on their bus 10 minutes before the bus could have possibly arrived on base. Welcome to Oz, Jimmy! I even kept from laughing at the things said and the antics of the drill instructors as they shouted at us in unison, trying to get everyone off the bus and onto a pair of yellow boot prints painted on the pavement near where we disembarked from the bus. Unfortunately, I only stayed "under the radar" for about thirty seconds after I put my feet on a pair of those yellow boot prints.

I got "dinged" on one of the drill instructor's radar screens and was noticed when a drill instructor yelled: "You puking maggots are pitiful!" For some reason I thought that was one of the most ridiculously funny things I had ever heard. A maggot is disgusting to me, but a puking maggot was just hilarious, I thought. After doing more push-ups, sit-ups and running in place than I thought possible, I was convinced that maybe it was not as funny as I first thought. We found out very quickly to never, ever commit the cardinal sin of looking directly at, or "eye-balling" a drill instructor. Retribution was swift, painful and embarrassing. The embarrassing part generally started with a drill instructor asking a recruit if the recruit was eye-balling him, followed by an innocent question like: "Do you like me?" No matter how a recruit answered it got worse. "Why do you like me?" or "Why do you not like me?" could be followed up with, "Are you queer for me?" or "You must be from Texas, all they have in Texas is steers and queers, right?" There was no way to escape their wrath and there was no right answer. The poor, wretched, recruit was utterly broken down to the lowest form of life on the planet. The world as we knew it was ending quickly. Welcome to Parris Island! Oorah!

Many a time I have thought back to my Parris Island boot camp experience. There is no doubt in my mind that everything that happened was orchestrated and carried out in a precise manner in order to make us Marines that followed orders instantly. Everything was confusing until we were able to sort it out in our minds that our world had been turned upside down and that we had better conform to our new world quickly or suffer the consequences. It all started that night when we got off the bus and placed our feet on the yellow boot prints. The sick humor exhibited by our drill instructors would have been really appreciated if it had not been at our expense. I figure they made sure that they caused a certain number of new recruits in our group to do or say something that would keep all of us busy exercising and running in place until the next little orchestrated event would take place. That next event started after we had exercised the rest of the night away. It would not be the last time that I did not notice time passing while I was in the Marines. They thoroughly had our attention! Just to make sure they had our attention we were paraded through a barbershop for the most painful and ugliest haircut any of us had probably ever experienced.

We proceeded to recruit receiving, turned in our orders and were assigned to a platoon. I was assigned to platoon 2006. The platoon was introduced to our three drill instructors in about the same manner as we were greeted at the bus, except in a more up close and personal manner. The drill instructors wanted to ensure that every member of the platoon knew that life as we knew it was over and that every second of every day for the next ten weeks would make hell look like a tropical paradise that we wished we could go to. They lined us up in a formation and fervently started teaching us how to march and run in proper order while on our way to get our basic issue of boots, clothing and toiletry items. We were given specific instructions on how to place all our civilian attire in a package to be mailed home. I remember mom telling me that when she received the package, she washed, ironed and stored the clothes in my closet. I love my mom. She was a real sweetheart. I also remember being really surprised when I went home on my first leave and put those same clothes on again. The pants were too loose and my shirt was too tight. I had lost an inch or so in the waist, plus had added some "beef" in my arms, chest and shoulders. Many things in your life can change in a very short time without you realizing it. Welcome to Marine boot camp! We ran, with all of our basic issue to our barracks, where we were assigned bunks and foot lockers. Thank goodness I was assigned a top bunk. They were easier to make up taunt, like the drill instructors liked. Little did I know that I would spend less time sleeping in my bunk than anyone else in my platoon. I will talk more about that issue later. We temporarily stored our basic issue and were hustled out of the barracks quickly to our next stop, medical examinations.

Our medical examinations were very thorough. We were weighed, measured, poked, probed and had our chests x-rayed. They checked our vision and hearing. They probably should have held off on the hearing until we graduated from boot camp. Ha! All of us would hear enough shouting and screaming in our ears to last ten life times. When the medical tests and exams were over, we received a real treat with our first battery of shots. When the United States Marine Corps mandates that every recruit shall be protected from every disease known to man, it is going to happen. We suffered through several batteries of shots during boot camp. Our Drill instructors were really empathetic to our plight. Yeah, right!

We were pretty sore after the shots, and even thought we might get a breather until the soreness wore off. Ha! Our drill instructors were waiting on us with one of their more perverse rounds of exercising. I think they really enjoyed making us do hundreds of pushups and sit-ups after getting shots, although I must admit it did take our minds off our sore arms and buttocks. After we had endured all we thought we could take, our drill instructors informed us that we were the next group to go to the mess hall. Hallelujah! I think each of us could have eaten a horse. Breakfast was being served. I could have sworn it had been days since my last meal, but then I realized that we had been here less than 12 hours. Once again time had passed without me having noticed. Go figure! Welcome to Oz, Jimmy!

Everyone should go through a Marine boot camp chow hall experience.

you march into the chow hall single file. You do not talk. You do not eye-ball chow hall attendants. You pick up trays and silverware in a prescribed manner, usually in a choreographed motion very rigidly defined by straight lines and right angles. Food is ladled or slopped onto your tray as you go through the "chow" line. You pick up your drink at the end of the chow line and go to your designated table. The food was basically okay and usually involved some form of spam at every meal. It was amazing how many ways they could prepare spam. Now-a-days I shy away from spam. I think I have had enough of it for one life time. Everyone performs the choreographed straight lines and right-angle eating motion in unison. Recruits eat and drink everything on their tray and in their cup or woe be to them. The drill instructors get great pleasure in correcting any mistake made, making everyone suffer for anyone's mistake. This experience would be repeated at every meal during boot camp. By the time we suffered through our first meal, our drill instructors had us believing we were pretty much the most worthless things known to mankind. Right about then, we were realizing that our boot camp experience would probably spiral downwards and get much worse before it got better. Semper Fi, Marine recruits!

Our drill instructors exhibited their wicked sense of humor over and over during boot camp. A good run punctuated with many stops for exercising was always in order after we had a good meal in our stomachs. The drill instructors continuously reminded us of our failings as we ran and marched, constantly pointing out our mistakes. The word walking was quickly expunged from our vocabulary. We ran, marched or marched double-time everywhere we went. Double-time march was basically a fast march. Marine recruits learned to march and to double-time march listening to our drill instructors' cadence. There were different marching movements and timing of movements to master and we mastered them before our boot camp experience was over. The discipline it took to follow our drill instructor's orders slowly crept into every fiber of our changing bodies and minds. Our bodies and minds were quickly adjusting to a new normal.

All of us were beginning to fear the wrath of our drill instructors. They got our attention quickly and over time the individual characteristics of our drill instructors became apparent to us. One of them was our father figure, one was our teacher figure and one was the enforcer. Staff sergeant Holmes was our father figure. I can still hear his melodic marching cadence in my mind.

Sergeant Gastol was our teacher figure. He would be everywhere shouting instructions and showing us how to do things. Sergeant O'Neil was our enforcer. Nothing got by him, real nor imagined. He reminded me of "Boo-Boo Bear" in the Yogi Bear comedies. I nicknamed him "Boo-Boo" and all of the platoon had a lot of fun out of saying: "Hey Boo-Boo" when he could not hear us. It caused us some pain when he caught on to us mocking him, but his nickname stuck with him all the way through boot camp. The platoon had to get some laughs somewhere, even if we had to do it on the sly. Amazingly, the sense of humor exhibited by the platoon was never broken by our drill instructors. We felt it really could not get any worse for us. What were they going to do, send us to Parris Island? This is not to say that only one of them would come down hard on us for the slightest transgression because all of them had eyes in the back of their heads that could spot a tiny thread out of place from unimaginable distances, hearing that could pick up the slightest noise from unbelievable distances, noses that could smell an infraction in a heart-beat and a sixth sense that was down-right spooky. They were well trained and experienced in training recruits. We had a lot to learn and we had better listen well, act accordingly or suffer our drill instructors' imaginative wrath. Welcome to Parris Island!

We double timed over to our Battalion armory where our quest to wear the "globe and anchor" and be recognized as a United States Marine started in earnest. We were issued our M-14 rifle, all the "782" gear we would need to go to war with and a galvanized bucket. These items were essential components needed in our marine boot camp training. Included in the "782" issue was a canteen, cup, cover, meat can (metal folding plate with handle), knapsack, haversack, shelter half, tent poles, pegs, web belt, straps, buckles and other assorted items needed to assemble field packs, including the light marching pack and field transport pack. All the gear we were issued that day was mind boggling. We had no idea what or how we would use all the items we were issued and would spend many anxious hours learning how to assemble and use our "782" gear. Everything we carried in the field was either attached to or placed inside a piece of "782" gear.

The galvanized metal bucket was a mystery to us when they issued it to us. We carried a lot of gear in it on our way back to our barracks and would soon learn it was a vital component of our training. I never realized a bucket could be used for so many things. Turn it upside down and you can sit on it, use it for a small table to set things on or write letters to your family on it. Put soap and water in it and you could wash your clothes, scrub the barracks floors or clean the head (bathroom). Carry it by the handle and you could carry things in it. The imagination of our drill instructors could really run wild with ideas on how to use our buckets. As a matter of fact, the imagination of our drill instructors could run wild on about any subject, usually at our expense!

With the issue of our M-14 rifle, we learned about a sacred United States Marine Corps tradition: "All Marines are riflemen!" All Marine recruits learn the rifle creed. It is as follows; This is my rifle. There are many like it but this one is mine. My rifle is my best friend. It is my life. I must master it as I master my life. I will…

My rifle, without me is useless. Without my rifle, I am useless. I must fire my rifle true. I must shoot straighter than my enemy who is trying to kill me. I must shoot him before he shoots me. I will…

My rifle and myself know that what counts in this war is not the rounds we fire, the noise of our burst, nor the smoke we make. We know that it is the hits that count. We will hit…

My rifle is human, even as I, because it is my life. Thus, I will learn it as a brother. I will learn its weakness, its strength, its parts, its accessories, its sights and its barrel. I will keep my rifle clean and ready, even as I am clean and ready. We will become part of each other. We will…

Before God I swear this creed. My rifle and myself are the defenders of my country. We are the masters of our enemy. We are the saviors of my life. So be it until victory is America's and there is no enemy, but peace! Semper Fi, Marine!

We memorized the rifle creed, our serial number and our rifle's serial number. Woe be to the Marine recruit who failed to memorize these three things in particular and many more things in general. Actually, it was pretty much woe be to any Marine recruit that failed to remember anything our drill instructors deemed worthy of us remembering. We were quickly learning that what they thought was worthy would come with a lot of hard work, blood, sweat and tears not only individually, but as a platoon. These are just a few of the things we would master over time during our boot camp experience. A lot of things happened to us that first day and we were tired and ready for some rest. We soon learned our barracks life was just another conduit of our training.

Our drill instructors really put us through the wringer when we got back to the barracks. We learned how to make our beds in the prescribed manner of the USMC. This took a little time, because our drill instructors loved to do all they could to make sure we would never forget the experience of failing to meet their standards for everything. When the bed making ordeal was over, we learned how and where to stow our gear and where to place our individual rifles in our barrack's rifle racks. Our drill instructors felt that our efforts fell short of their expectations and proceeded to tear all of the bedding off our beds, empty our footlockers and in general create mayhem. When we finally met their expectations, they decided that our barracks area was filthy and needed to be cleaned immediately.

Only a drill instructor could make this a teaching moment by pointing out that the United States Marine Corps had issued us a bucket and we were ignoring our buckets by not using them. We were ordered to put our buckets over our heads and to beat on them with our United States Marine Corps issue brush while running in place. After several minutes of this teaching moment, the moral of the story became apparent. We should never disrespect the wisdom of the United States Marine Corps and embarrass our drill instructors by not using every piece of equipment issued to us. We were ordered to put water in our buckets and to scrub every square inch of the floors in the barracks and head area with our United States Marine Corps issue brush. This was a very tiring endeavor and our drill instructors used every moment to discipline the platoon for any infraction committed by any member of the platoon. Just another of the many bonding moments we as a platoon would learn to suffer together. Individuality was rapidly disappearing and we were starting to bond as a platoon. Semper Fi! At last we were able to take a shower and crawl in bed, we thought. Silly us! We had soiled our barracks and head again. The punishment for that was to clean the barracks and head again. I must admit, it was easier the second time. Finally, we were allowed to hit the sack…but not all of us.

Our barracks was a wooden, two story structure with two squad bay areas on each deck. The barracks pre-dated World War II. Each squad bay was assigned to a different platoon. Platoons had their own sleeping area with associated heads, utility closets, rifle racks and on duty drill instructor quarters. Every Marine recruit barracks at Parris Island posted a fire watch within each squad bay at night. The duty of each recruit walking fire watch was to immediately alert his drill instructor and platoon about any fire or smoke observed anywhere in the barracks. An additional duty was to go to your drill instructors' quarters at the prescribed time set by your drill instructor, slap the frame of his door three times and shout; "Sir, the time on deck is zero whatever the prescribed time is, Sir!" That first night I was assigned the last fire watch with the dubious duty of awakening our Drill instructor. I mentioned earlier in this story that I did not get to sleep a full night during my whole boot camp experience. Probably had something to do with an ornery streak in me. I can proudly say that they never got that ornery streak out of me, but I paid a price. Semper Fi, Jimmy!

I was tired and sore when I was awakened to walk my turn at fire watch. I got dressed and proceeded to walk around the barracks, rifle rack area and head. Occasionally, I would see another recruit on fire watch from one of the other squad bays and nod at him. We did not dare to speak for fear of waking one of our drill instructors. At the prescribed time, I went to my drill instructor's door, slammed the palm of my hand three times on the door frame, shaking the entire squad bay, and yelled at the top of my lungs; "Sir the time on deck is zero whatever the time was, Sir!" Wow! Did I ever get a response, and not only from my drill instructor! He and the other drill instructors apparently slept in their clothes with boots on, because all four of them exploded out of their respective platoon squad bay rooms like hornets out of a nest stinging me with their yelling and screaming. I could not believe what I was seeing and hearing. It was like I had stuck a stick in a hornet's nest. Two of those drill instructors came up the stairs from the lower deck squad bays and were yelling at me before the two drill instructors from our deck could get to me. All I knew to do was to stand at attention, bite my tongue and try not to smile or laugh. When they finished yelling and screaming at me, three of them went to their squad bays and my drill instructor had me start doing pushups and sit-ups. Did I know how to get noticed or what? Welcome to Parris Island!

I felt our drill instructor was getting a bit bored with me because he was looking towards the squad bay. Somewhere in our squad bay someone giggled and his bat like instincts had zeroed in on the noise. Oh boy! If I had not disturbed all the hornets in the nest, that giggle definitely did. Our drill instructor flipped on our squad bay lights, kicked one of our trash cans across the squad bay floor and commenced to yell and scream at everyone to get out of bed and start doing pushups and sit-ups. It is amazing how quick exercising can wipe out giggles and get you serious. When he had our attention, we practiced standing at attention and barking "yes sir" and "no sir" to his instructions. Finally, we were allowed to use the head, wash up, shave, make up our beds, clean up the barracks and get ready to fall out, which basically meant to line up outside in a platoon sized formation.

This pattern would repeat itself every day for the rest of boot camp. We immediately began to learn different commands, what the commands meant and how to follow commands without question or hesitation. When forming up in formation, we usually lined up in four equal lines with equal distance between the recruit in front of you, behind you and next to you, everyone facing in the same direction. Most of the time we had our rifles with us. We marched with our rifles and we ran with our rifles. Our rifles became a part of us. We learned the manual of arms and repeated the moves associated with the manual of arms over and over and over and over until we mastered the manual of arms. There were many things we had to master, and our drill instructors were there to ensure that we did, never losing their zeal to correct us in imaginative ways that usually involved exercising or running sprinkled with colorful words to ensure they had our attention.

Learning the intricate commands, cadences and orchestrated moves associated with marching was a major part of our boot camp experience. Our drill instructors were master teachers. We learned to march in cadence and double time march in cadence. As we mastered moves and commands our drill instructors would teach us more, increasing their instructions until after weeks of marching, we became an integrated platoon that wordlessly and effortlessly flowed with the rhythm of the cadence and commands. To this day I can still hear our drill instructors' cadences and feel the rhythm and flow of marching. I went back to Parris Island a few years ago with my wife, Kathy. Watching a well-trained platoon of Marine Recruits march was a real treat. Kathy wondered why some recruits were being yelled at and treated so harshly by their drill instructors. I explained to her that everything she was watching was an orchestrated effort to make Marines out of the recruits and was all a part of their training. After watching different platoons in different phases of their training, she finally understood the importance of the frenzy of the training and the antics of the drill instructors. She wondered if the recruits ever got a break.

I told her that every day the routine was rigorous and appeared to be non-stop, but there were breaks. After training, cleaning up our barracks, equipment and ourselves there was a little time to write letters and quietly visit. Usually we visited while we were cleaning our clothes, equipment or shining our boots and shoes. We usually had a "mail call" time at night after everything settled down. Our drill instructor would climb on top of a table that was located in the center of our squad bay, order us to stand at attention in front of our bunks and call out our names if we had mail. Getting mail or packages could be a good experience or a bad experience, usually bad. If a letter didn't have any extraneous items in it and it did not have a perfume or other smell, mail call could be a good experience. When a letter obviously had something in it or if it had a smell, mail call could be a bad experience. When someone received a letter that had a smell, such as perfume, the drill instructor would ask the recruit receiving the letter if the recruit loved his drill instructors. We had already gone through the "do you like me-love me" routine when we got off the bus and stepped on the yellow boot prints. You must realize that all drill instructors adhere to the mantra of no recruit is capable of answering a drill instructor's question properly. Any answer led to more questions and each question got the recruit deeper in the drill instructor's wrath. It was a really bad experience. After you suffered through it, you wrote home and informed your loved ones what kind of letter to send in the future. Welcome to Parris Island! Ha!

My mom always sent small packs of peanuts or kool-aid in her letters to me. After suffering through the drill instructor's questions, I would have to open the package of peanuts, count them and make sure I gave every recruit a peanut, even if I had to split each peanut with the drill instructor's knife. Usually, every recruit would be lined up in single file and march around the barracks with each recruit reporting to the drill instructor in front of the table while I would place a peanut in each recruit's hand. We had to rigidly adhere to the orchestrated straight lines and right angles when we placed the peanuts in our mouths. My drill instructor really enjoyed it when I received kool-aid in the mail. Fortunately, it did not happen but two or three times. He would order me to get up on his table while he opened the pack and poured it into my mouth and then dare me to spit any of it out.   If you have never tried pouring a pack of kool-aid in your mouth, do not try it.   It was bad!   I thought I was going to choke to death.   I finally got mom to stop sending me pokie bait (junk food) in my letters while I was in boot camp.   God bless her!   I love my mom.

My aunt Judy nearly out did my mom when she sent me a giant box of her home-made brownies.   Aunt Judy made great brownies, but boot camp was not the place to get them in the mail.   Needless to say, I was back up on the table again stuffing brownies in my mouth and woe be if I dropped a crumb on the drill instructor's table or on the deck.   Sergeant Gastol was on duty that night and he actually cut me some slack by lining everyone up and marching them up to the table one by one for a piece of brownie.   Trust me, it could have been much worse for me if not for that small act of kindness. He made up for it by having everyone clean the barracks again before we were allowed to hit the sack.   Fortunately for me there had been some others that had received packages that night or the platoon would have been pretty upset with me.   I love my aunt Judy!

As the days and weeks went by, our drill instructors introduced us to physical training, strength tests, the confidence (obstacle) course, swimming, the pugil stick, bayonet training, hand to hand combat, conditioning hikes, guard duty, the rifle and pistol ranges, mess duty, and various classes where we learned military courtesy, tent pitching, and pretty much all the basic things we would need to know as Marines.   Our progress was measured with drill competitions, physical readiness tests, a field meet and fun filled Elliot's beach, where we displayed our knowledge in all of the above.   We competed against other platoons for guide iron ribbons (streamers) as we mastered different phases.   All of this would prepare us for our final inspection and graduation.

Our physical training increased daily.   I never thought I could do so many pushups, pull-ups, sit-ups, thrusts, leg lifts and other exercises in one day.   We would hold buckets of sand away from our bodies, arms stretched out until we could not hold them up any longer.   We held our rifles with our arms stretched out in front of us or over our heads until we thought our arms would fall off. We raced in platoon size and individual hundred-yard races until we thought our legs and bodies could not take any more. We ran for miles and miles at a time. Just when we thought we could do no more, we would repeat everything all over again. New challenges to our strength and stamina were added daily in addition to our regular exercises and running. I must admit, we were in excellent shape when we left Parris Island.

We learned that a confidence course was exactly what it said it was. When we first saw some of the climbing towers, rope towers, monkey bars, mud, water and sand pits, we figured we were really in for it. We went from climbing up and down ropes and obstacles to racing up and down ropes and obstacles in all kind of conditions. To add a little reality, sand, water and mud played a part in many of the obstacles. It was impressive how many ways ropes and obstacles could be used to punish our bodies, but we grew stronger and stronger and met each challenge head on. A lot of bruises, scrapes and hard landings were suffered before we mastered every obstacle thrown at us. We were learning that our bodies could take much more punishment than any of us ever dreamed our bodies could. Our confidence in ourselves was growing daily. Just as soon as our confidence was built up, our drill instructors would introduce us to another phase of training.

Amphibious operations are an integral part of the United States Marine Corps. Therefore, all Marines should know how to swim and should understand water survival techniques. Our swimming phase of recruit training started with a platoon sized plunge into a large, indoor pool. If a recruit could not swim, that recruit would get a crash course in how to swim. After ensuring that all of us could swim, drill instructors taught us how to survive in the water. Their ingenious methods bordered on torture. They loved to poke you with a pole in the back of the head when they felt your technique was not up to par. We conducted water survival training in bathing suits or with our utility uniforms on, with and without boots. It was very challenging. We were taught different types of artificial respiration and lifesaving methods. In order to show that we had mastered water survival we had to prove to our drill instructors that we could survive in open water, without touching the bottom or sides of the pool, for whatever time our drill instructor's thought was adequate, which seemed like hours. I remember counting the squares on the bottom of the pool. We all had to pass, or no one passed, so we would encourage each other to hang in there. We eventually mastered the swimming phase and moved on to our next phase of training.

Pugil stick, bayonet and hand to hand combat training were challenging. This phase of training was not as tortuous as I thought it would be, at least to me. Probably had something to do with my ornery streak. Basically, all three evolved around boxing techniques. As we mastered our technique with the pugil stick, the bayonet and hand to hand combat training became easier. The pugil stick is basically a stick with padded ends that you knocked your opponent on the ground with or "out pointed" him with. You got scored by the correct contact blows you landed to your opponent's body. If your technique was lacking, you could get beat up pretty good. Fortunately, we wore pads and a helmet. Pugil stick training helped us master the use of our bayonets. Our pugil stick technique helped us deliver and parry blows from our opponents. On the bayonet course, we combined technique with aggression. A good technique, combined with tempered aggressiveness, could be the difference in life or death in a close encounter with the enemy. Hand to hand fighting was made a lot easier because of our new found aggressiveness and confidence in our fighting abilities. We learned self-defense techniques, how to control our body, how to fall without injuring ourselves, and how to use our opponent's weaknesses, strengths and weight to disable them. In addition to technique, we learned what part of our opponent's body to attack and how to defend ourselves against knife attacks. Our drill instructors constantly reminded us that to survive, we must render our opponent helpless. Pugil stick, bayonet and hand to hand training really instilled confidence in our ability to fend off our opponent and survive a fight. Fortunately, I never had to use my bayonet nor my hand to hand combat skills in combat in Vietnam. Thank you, Lord!

Every now and then a disagreement would take place between one recruit or another resulting in a fight. Usually when this happened, our drill instructors would give boxing gloves to the recruits that were fighting and instruct the rest of the platoon to form a circle around the fighters. The drill instructors would make the recruits fight until they felt the fighters were worn out. It is amazing how heavy those gloves would get! After the fight we usually paid a price as a platoon for the fighter's transgression of order with a good dose of calisthenics or a punishing run with our rifles in our outstretched arms or held above our heads. When recruits caused the platoon to suffer unnecessarily, we had a way of correcting their attitudes that usually took care of any future attitude problems. Some may think our methods were cruel, but they worked.

Early in our training, our drill instructors picked a group of us to render "off the books" discipline to any recruit that would not get with the program or had a bad attitude. We would talk to the recruit individually or as a group, counseling him to get his act together. If the recruit refused to listen, we would try a more aggressive approach by surrounding his bunk after he had gone to sleep, holding him under his blankets and beating him with socks filled with soap bars. If that did not work, the recruit would be counseled by the drill instructors and if it appeared there was an irreconcilable problem, the recruit would be dropped from our platoon for special training. This only happened once or twice, although we did have one guy that probably should have been dropped from our platoon because he really struggled to stay up with everyone. Sometimes the drill instructors had him sit in the utility closet on his bucket. I do not know how he slipped through the recruiting system nor why they let him complete boot camp. Scuttlebutt was they found him a job as a shoe cobbler after boot camp. Good for him!

Our next training phase was at the rifle and pistol ranges. We moved out of our barracks and into the rifle range barracks. The rifle range barracks were relatively new, brick barracks designed basically like our old barracks, except bigger and nicer. Upon arrival at the rifle range, we started learning the four basic rifle firing positions used at the firing range and we practiced "snapping-in" with our rifles. The purpose of snapping-in was to teach proper firing position techniques and to train our muscles to accept the tight rifle sling adjustments. At first, our arms and legs resisted the sling adjustments and firing positions, but gradually our muscles accepted the punishment even to the point of feeling pretty comfortable while in our firing positions. We learned rifle range safety rules, proper trigger squeeze, how to use our score book, how to use our rifle's elevation and windage adjustments and how to align our sights so our bullet would hit the "Bull's-Eye" or the black center of the target.

We were all excited and a little bit nervous the first day we actually started firing our rifles down range at targets. Some of us would be on the firing line and others would be in the butt area handling the targets. When we were on butt detail, we would haul targets up and down in their respective target carriages. The targets were in line with a firing station on the firing line. Each firing station was numbered and had a corresponding target butt. Recruits manning the butt detail were protected by a concrete wall with soil piled in front of it. The concrete wall had a concrete overhang that the butt detail stood under when the other recruits were firing. Every recruit strived to hit the target's bull's-eye with every shot in order to obtain a high score. Different numbered, concentric white circles, outlined in black, radiated away from the bull's-eye. The object was to hit the bull's-eye or hit as close to the bull's-eye as we could place our shot. Hitting the bull's-eye would really get us excited and it was imperative that we learned to control our excitement. When a shot was fired at the target, we were responsible for, we would pull the target down and mark where the shot hit the target with a white or black dowel marker. A white dowel was used on black areas of the target and a black dowel was used on white areas of the target. This allowed the recruit firing at the target to observe where he hit the target, record where he hit the target in his score book and to adjust his sights, if needed. If the shot did not hit the target, we would wave a red flag or disc in the air in front of his target. We called this a "Maggie's Drawers." After each shot, we repeated the above procedure until the recruit finished firing.

The most exciting time at boot camp for me was when I fired down range at my target. I worked really hard to learn my elevation and windage at the different firing stations. We fired from the one-hundred-yard firing line, the two-hundred-yard firing line, the three-hundred-yard firing line and the five-hundred-yard firing line. It was imperative that we learned what our elevation and windage was from each firing position. We called this getting the "dope" right on our rifles. We also called this 'zeroing in" our rifles. It taught us the importance of knowing that we could hit what we were aiming at with our rifles. If we messed this up during our practice rounds it would keep us from firing a high score on qualification day and on the battle field it could cost us our lives. There were four grades when you qualified; expert, sharpshooter, marksman or unqualified. Every Marine strives to shoot expert. It is a mark of honor. I earned my expert badge twice and a sharpshooter badge once while on active duty in the Marines. Like I said earlier, if you are not prepared to give one hundred per cent, it is going to be hard to succeed and accomplish your dreams. I was really disappointed with that sharpshooter badge, but no one forced me to party hard and late the night before qualification.

I worked really hard during my practice rounds and listened intently to what my marksmanship coach told me. On one of my practice rounds, I was struggling a bit and my marksmanship coach got my attention by placing one of my left fingers in my rifle receiver and let the bolt slide down on my finger. Wow! That got my attention quickly. Boy did that hurt. Must have helped because I never lost my concentration after that. On qualification day I was really excited. There was no doubt in my mind that I would fire expert, I just did not know how high my score would be. Our drill instructors and my marksmanship coach had definitely instilled confidence in me. I was pumped! When I saw that first dowel in the bull's-eye I wanted to jump up and celebrate. I kept hitting the bull's-eye at the one-hundred-yard firing line, the two-hundred-yard firing line and at the three-hundred-yard firing line. At the five-hundred-yard firing line, I missed the bull's-eye with the first and second shots. I nearly panicked, but then I calmed myself down, checked my dope on the rifle, re-set the windage and elevation and started hitting the bull's-eye again. I shot high expert! That night at our barracks, everyone that shot expert was given some pokey bait (junk food) and free time while everyone else cleaned the barracks. We really thought we were something special that night. The rest of the platoon ignored us or heckled us. We knew that they really admired our accomplishment. This euphoria lasted until the next morning and then our regular routine of marching, performing the manual of arms, exercising, running and catching our drill instructor's wrath started back up with a fury.

The pistol range was not as complex and demanding as the rifle range. There was not as much to learn about the pistol as there was to learn about the rifle. For some reason, I thought the pistol range was more dangerous than the rifle range. It was fun learning how to disassemble, clean and reassemble the forty-five-caliber automatic pistol. All of the pistols we qualified with had pretty worn out barrels, making it hard to fire a tight group of shots. We did not qualify for a badge for some reason. I really think it was because they knew the pistol barrels were worn out or it could have been because in 1967, the Marines scaled back boot camp from thirteen weeks to ten weeks, probably because of Vietnam. We were reminded over and over about weapon safety and about how dangerous training can be by our drill instructors. While at the pistol range, we saw an ambulance go to the rifle range. It was rumored some idiot had grabbed the top of the concrete overhang in the butt area, pulled himself up and stuck his head up over the concrete. We also heard about a recruit accidentally shooting himself in the head while at the pistol range. Those two recruits probably did not survive their mistakes. These accidents really brought home the danger of forgetting your weapon safety training.

While we were at the rifle range barracks and after we had qualified with our rifles and mastered the pistol, we were informed that it was our turn for mess hall duty. Every recruit platoon had to pull one week of mess hall duty. Our week of mess hall duty went by pretty quick with relatively few glitches. Several of us managed to sneak extra food, including cookies and desserts back to the barracks without getting caught. After the on-duty drill instructor went to sleep we would have a quiet party. We nearly got caught once but managed to avoid detection. Just before we started mess hall duty a recruit that had dropped out of his platoon after his rifle range phase because of sickness, joined our platoon. He was an African American recruit from Detroit with a big racist chip on his shoulder. He immediately alienated himself from everyone, including the other African American recruits because of his bad attitude. The platoon was on edge because he would cause grief every chance he got, usually at someone else's expense. Fortunately, it all came to a head quickly and with a good ending.

I had a few words with him about his attitude and he did not like it. He started running his mouth off at me and threatening me, especially while at work in the mess hall. I tried to ignore him, but it all came to a head when he tripped me while I was carrying a tray of bacon to the serving line. I came up off that floor and hit him as hard as I have hit anyone in my life and actually stunned him. If I would have stopped and walked off, he probably would have been the only one to get in trouble, but I hit him again and that just snapped him out of his shock from the first hit. We proceeded to get into a real hum dinger of a fight that I wished I had not started. He waxed me pretty good before they stopped the fight and pulled us apart. I told him to get ready, because he was going to have to fight me every-day he woke up in boot camp. Some of the other platoon members, including the other African American platoon members told him the same thing and that everyone was through with his sorry attitude.

That night at the barracks, the drill instructors really had a field day with us. They told us how worthless we were and then had all of us stand under the cold water in the shower with our uniforms on until we nearly turned blue. That incident probably pulled us together as a platoon more than anything else during boot camp. The recruit from Detroit had a one hundred eighty degree turn around in attitude. He changed and improved so much after that night that he was well liked by all of us by the end of boot camp. He even held the highest honor in our platoon, the position of right guide when in formation. Boot camp probably helped shape the attitude of that recruit from Detroit for the rest of his life. I hope he is still alive and has had a successful, happy life. I think that fight with him is one of the reasons my jaw bugs me to this day, that and possibly a few other fights here and there. Ha!

Learning how to report to a superior in our chain of command and how to stand guard duty were particular items our drill instructors wanted us to master. Adhering to customs and courtesies are essential to every Marine, from a recruit to the Commandant of the United States Marine Corps. Forgetting a custom or courtesy could cause a recruit serious problems. We really worked hard to not embarrass our drill instructors in front of a superior in our chain of command. Our platoon suffered many hours of punishment for failures in customs and courtesies, but by the end of boot camp we were well versed in them. One of the quaint customs was to not smile while having your official USMC picture taken. When it was my turn to have my official USMC picture taken, I suffered a bout of the giggles, followed by a spasm of uncontrolled laughter. Needless to say, this caused other recruits to smile or laugh. This was viewed as tantamount to failure of discipline and order and was totally unacceptable to our drill instructors. It took over an hour of yelling, threatening, exercising and running before our drill instructors got us in what they felt was a more Marine like composure where we could finish having our pictures taken. After the picture taking was over, our drill instructors really put us through the wringer. Several of us thought it was worth the punishment just to see the total flabbergasted look on Boo Boo's face. His mouth was moving, but no sound came out of his mouth. Thank the Lord for our drill instructors getting all of us in tip top physical shape. We needed every ounce of strength we could muster to get through what they put us through that day.

As boot camp started to wind down, we were issued complete sets of United States Marine Corps uniforms that were meticulously tailored to fit each of us. Our drill instructors made sure they were "ship-shape" down to the last button and thread. An out of place thread was called an "Irish Pennant" and there was absolutely no excuse for a missing button or a button that was not in proper alignment with your uniform. We learned early in boot camp that the United States Marine Corps was very serious about the condition of our uniforms and equipment. Our drill instructors really wanted us to look sharp. We put in a lot of time and effort polishing our leather and brass to a sparkling finish. The creases ironed into our uniforms looked like they were honed by a whetstone. There was no excuse for a sloppily turned out Marine!

Boot camp started to wind down after Elliot's Beach. At Elliot's Beach we lived in the boonies, ate our meals outside with our mess kits that had been issued to us and slept under our tents. We were given proficiency tests to see if we had mastered what we had been taught up to that time. We learned first aid procedures and techniques. We took conditioning hikes with full packs, rifle and gear. In general, we learned how to survive in the field using our equipment and skills. We had one last physical readiness test where we ran the obstacle course, climbed ropes, ran in formation and practiced the "fireman's carry." The fireman's carry basically is a method used to carry another Marine over your shoulder to first aid or safety.

Before graduation, we competed against other platoons in a field meet and drill competition. The field meet was a lot of fun because I liked to run and I could run fast. I ran the first leg of our relay race. Our platoon took first place in the field meet. I came in third overall in pull-ups and first overall in sit-ups. We were proud of our first-place ribbon (streamer). Drill competition was tough. We had to show that we had mastered all the commands, moves and cadences. I made a monumental mistake on one of the moves. I stepped out with the wrong foot, standing out of line like a sore thumb when the command was given to turn and stop. Luckily for me I remembered what our drill instructors had taught us about getting caught out of place. I stayed perfectly still and at attention until the next command was given and then I stepped back in place. We made fewer mistakes than the other platoons and won the first-place ribbon (streamer). We won more first-place ribbons (streamers) than any of the other platoons we competed against and earned the right to be named the "Honor Platoon." All of us were pretty proud of that.

Finally, the end was in sight! We had a final inspection where our entire chain of command inspected every recruit from "stem to stern" and asked us questions about everything we had learned during our recruit training, including our rifles and Marine customs and courtesies. I answered all of my questions correctly, thank goodness. After final inspection, we marched over to the battalion armory and turned in our rifles and other gear that we would not take with us to our next duty station. The night before graduation was a flurry of activity. We had to polish our brass, polish our shoes, get our uniforms ship shape and pack our uniforms and personal items in our sea bags. Our drill instructors talked to us individually and collectively, pointing out things we needed to do, basically settling us down. They were very calming. We even thought we would miss them and the frenzy of boot camp. Yeah, right! All of us were starting to understand what we had gone through and our chests were swelling with pride. We had taken everything thrown at us, earning the right to be called a United States Marine and wear the globe and anchor. I was really excited because I realized that my childhood dream was about to come true.

The morning of graduation day was a busy time. Our drill instructors pointed out where to stage our gear that was to be loaded on the buses that would take us to Camp Geiger, North Carolina after graduation ceremonies. When we lined up in formation to march to the drill field for our graduation ceremony, we were really excited. Our drill instructors showed us off to everyone watching by having us perform different close order drill moves we had mastered. Everyone looked good and performed our close order drill moves thinking that no other recruit platoon could come close to looking as good as us. When we got to the drill grounds, we stood in formation while the ceremony began. I caught a glimpse of my mom in the stands and much to my surprise, my dad was there. I could not believe it. Unbeknownst to me, they had decided to get back together and wanted to combine a vacation with attending my boot camp graduation. Finally, the ceremony started and mercifully it did not last long. The fury of boot camp was finally over. Oorah! Marine Corps!

When Sergeant Gastol pinned my globe and anchor on the lapels of my tunic I realized I had become what I had wished for as a young boy. I was officially a United States Marine. I had been tested and I had passed. Sergeant Gastol interrupted my reverie by telling me he thought I needed a couple more weeks of training at Parris Island. That brought me back down to the ground and quick. He was smiling and I was hoping he was kidding me. He had me worried there for a second. I thought I was on his good side because earlier in the day, a supply truck, traveling down the street in front of our barracks too fast, dropped a box with a pair of dress shoes in it. I picked up the box of shoes and gave it to Sergeant Gastol. They happened to be his size. I told him that I had tried to get the truck driver's attention but could not. He told me to not look a gift horse in the mouth and thanks.

After our graduation ceremony, I took mom and dad around the base and showed them our barracks and where we had trained. I could not show them the rifle range and some other areas because of restrictions, but they got a good look at Parris Island. They told me about them getting back together and I told them I was proud for them. We ate at the base cafeteria. Recruits were not allowed base privileges during training. It was kind of nice to be allowed privileges that other Marines enjoyed. We had a great visit, but it was cut short because I had to get on a bus to Camp Geiger for advanced infantry training. We said our good-byes. I told them I would write them as soon as I got settled and that I would be able to go home on leave after I finished my four or five weeks of training at Camp Geiger. As our buses left Parris Island, we were excited about what our infantry training at camp Geiger would be like.

PLATOON 2006
HONOR PLATOON   M.C.R.D., PARRIS ISLAND, S.C.

SECOND RECRUIT BATTALION   SSGT. L. HOLMES   SGT. T.F. O'NEILL
SGT. J.C. GASTON   GRADUATED 12 - SEPT. - 1967

3

Camp Geiger

Early on, during boot camp, we spent a day taking aptitude tests, both written and oral. Our civilian experience, ability to comprehend things and any skills we happened to possess were analyzed. Based on our interviews, tests and abilities, a determination was made as to what military occupation skill might be compatible to each of us. Future duty assignments would depend on what our military occupation skill was. The vast majority of us would be assigned to infantry occupation skills. After all, every Marine is a rifleman! My assigned occupational skill when I graduated boot camp and reported to the infantry training school at Camp Geiger was an infantry rifleman, while I was in the Marines, my assigned duties would range from rifleman to grenadier, fire team and squad leader, prison guard, military policeman, corporal of the guard and sergeant of the guard.

We arrived at Camp Geiger with none of the noise and fanfare associated with our arrival at Parris Island. Our training instructors were waiting on us as we pulled up next to our barracks and they gave us instructions, pointing out where we needed to go and what we needed to do. A tough looking Marine gunnery sergeant advised us that a good infantryman should learn to observe, listen and adapt. He told us to pay close attention to what our instructors teach us during infantry training and to be very serious about how we apply ourselves during training. The gunny told us that what we learned and how we paid attention during infantry training could save our lives and the lives of other Marines. He pointed out that live rounds and blanks were used during infantry training and that we could be hurt or possibly killed while participating in "live fire" training exercises. He also pointed out that many of our instructors had recently returned from combat in Vietnam and were not only well versed in Marine infantry tactics, but were also well versed in the tactics used by the Viet Cong (V.C.) and the north Vietnamese Army (N.V.A.)

against Marines in Vietnam.

The gunny definitely got our attention. We were assigned bunks, wall lockers and foot lockers. We went to the battalion armory and were issued M-1 rifles with bayonets along with all of the "782" gear we would need during training. After storing our gear and locking our rifles in rifle racks, we were given a quick orientation of the base, told where we were allowed to go during training and where we were not allowed to go. We could not drink alcoholic beverages, nor could we get passes to go off base. They kept us on a pretty tight leash. We would soon realize why they kept us on a tight leash as our training progressed. Pretty much every minute was tied up in our training schedule. We had a lot to learn and a short time to learn it. Once again, like in boot camp, the pressure was slowly being ratcheted up. Oorah! Marine Corps!

As usual, all Marine training starts with marches, running and exercises. Our conditioning hikes and forced marches were considerably longer than any marches we had previously completed in boot camp. Many miles would be marched before our training was over. Some of our training areas were too far away to march and still have enough time to train. When that would happen, they took us to the training sites in what we called "cattle cars." Basically, a cattle car was a trailer hooked up to a truck. They packed us in tight, like sardines. There was no heating nor air conditioning and the cattle cars were very uncomfortable. Needless to say, we were usually more than ready to get out of the cattle cars. We were quickly learning that if there was a hard way for the Marines to do something, then why worry with an easy way of doing something. Such was the way of the United States Marine Corps. Because of these little idiosyncrasies, we were learning Marine euphemisms used by Marine infantrymen the world over like; "The Crotch" instead of the Marines Corps or if we knew we were getting the short end of the stick we would say that we were getting the "Green Weenie." Every infantryman from the beginning of time probably had nicknames or euphemisms for their respective armies. Actually, we would realize that because of doing everything the hard way, we would appreciate the easy way. It was this dichotomy of life as a United States Marine infantryman that became second nature to me and quite frankly, has stuck with me throughout my life. I strongly feel that this inculcated dichotomy is also why I am alive today and have that "Jimmy" look my family accuses me of having. Ha!

Another difference appreciably noticed was that we could eat our meals at a "mess hall" and not have to worry about the choreographed routine we had to follow at boot camp "chow halls." The food selection was a lot better and we actually had a choice of different things to eat. We were usually on a tight time schedule, but eating your meals was a lot more pleasurable than boot camp. There was generally plenty of milk, tea, coffee, kool-aid and fruit drinks available at meals. During most of our training at Camp Geiger, we ate our meals in the field training areas at a field mess facility or were issued "C" rations. Even then, the food was pretty good. For eating utensils, we used our field mess kits or the metal trays provided at the field mess facility. I remember the first time I used a metal tray at a field mess facility. When you finished your meal, the hottest barrel of water you have ever witnessed was used to rinse your tray. We learned to be very careful cleaning those trays and our field mess kits. That water would scald you for life!

The "C" rations they would issue us usually had cans of a prepared meal like ham and butterbeans, chicken soup with vegetables, and other meat-meal combinations. Actually, the "C" rations were not that bad. Several meat-meal combinations were offered. Cans of fruit, a can with crackers, a small can of peanut butter, chocolate candy, cigarettes, chewing gum and other items were also in the "C" ration box. I learned to squirrel away plenty of tobasco sauce every chance I got to "enhance" the taste of some of the meals. The kool-aid my mom would send me in her letters was put to good use mixing it with the water I had in my canteens. I started putting kool-aid in my canteens at Camp Geiger and pretty much continued that practice while I was in the Marines. Thank you, mom! She was a jewel.

Our training was overwhelming and very intense. We really had to pay attention. There was so much to learn and we could feel the intensity building every day. At first, I do not think it dawned on us why this was, but slowly it started to sink in that in less than three months we would be experiencing the real thing, mortal combat with an enemy that shoots back! It should have been a sobering thought, yet none of us thought anything could stop us. Our bodies were tougher than steel and we were becoming a well-trained fighting machine. Oh boy, did all of us ever have a rude awakening coming our way in a reality check named Vietnam. Oorah! Marine Corps!

Training included individual, fire team, squad, platoon, company and battalion tactics. A fire team is made up of four marines, usually with a corporal or lance corporal in charge of the fire team. A squad is made up of three fire teams, a Navy medical corpsman, a radio operator, any attached heavy weapons crews and a squad leader. Usually, the squad leader is a sergeant. A platoon is made up of three squads, any attached heavy weapons crews, one or two platoon radio operators, a platoon right guide or a platoon sergeant, a platoon leader, and sometimes an artillery/aircraft forward observer. Usually, a platoon sergeant is a staff sergeant and a platoon leader a second or first lieutenant. Heavy weapons usually were machine guns and mortars. Heavy weapons squads sometimes had their own squad leader and radio operators. A company is made up of three infantry platoons with a heavy weapons platoon, company radio operators and company headquarters staff. Usually, a company commander is a captain sometimes assisted by a first lieutenant, as company executive officer and a company gunnery sergeant. A battalion is made up of three infantry companies, a weapons company, and a headquarters company. Usually, the battalion commander is a colonel or lieutenant colonel assisted by a lieutenant colonel or major as the executive officer, several lieutenants, a sergeant major, first sergeant, gunnery sergeant, staff sergeants, sergeants and others as necessary.

We learned how to attack various kinds of emplacements, how to set up different fields of fire to enhance the efficiency of our fire power, how to conduct a patrol, how to set up ambushes, how to land navigate using a compass and map, and how to dig and use fox holes and other emplacements. Weapons training and maintenance included familiarization with individual and crew served weapons and using various types of firing ranges to test our skills with different weapons and firing scenarios.

At first, the myriad tactics and movements used by an infantry unit in the field or in combat were perplexing. As we gained confidence through repetition, we started acting as a unit and the various tactics made sense. Our individual tactics were really no more than realizing we were a part of the whole, although there could be a time when you were isolated and it was up to you to maintain self-discipline in order to survive by improvising, adapting and overcoming. We learned how to advance under fire in squad or fire team leap frog movements where one squad or fire team would advance while the other two squads or fire teams laid down covering fire. We learned how to use encircling movements and on-line assaults against an entrenched enemy using overwhelming fire power.

Sometimes we would be the enemy force and try to ambush Marines on patrol or in emplacements. One night we were designated an enemy force and were instructed to attack Marine forces in emplacements. After a night of continuous attacks, we were allowed to go to our fox holes and catch some sleep. We were really worn out and practically fell into our holes asleep. Early the next morning as we heard our sergeant's orders to form up, we woke up with some surprises in our hole, snakes. Needless to say, we got out of those holes quick! I had some blank rounds left and shot a couple of the snakes at close range. It is amazing what a blank round can do to a snake at close range. I got a pretty good chewing out by one of the sergeants for shooting the blank rounds at the snakes and all of our excess blank rounds were confiscated. Oh well, what are they going to do? Send us to Vietnam? As I have stated, I never lost my ornery streak.

I contracted strep throat and it laid me low for two or three days with a high fever. I felt that something was not right with me before I passed out on the ground after a long, stifling cattle car ride. I was sent to sick bay. Fortunately for me, I was allowed to make up the training time I missed. They let me make up the training time I missed over the next couple of weeks during my free time. What the heck, I did not need any free time anyway. Oorah! Marine Corps! Dad gum crotch could slip the green weenie to you at any time. Semper Fi, Marines!

I do not think anyone liked the tear gas training session. Only a sadistic, crazy son of gun would want to put on a gas mask after walking into a tear gas chamber for training purposes. Duh! Our instructors really got a kick out of watching us heaving, gagging and tearing up with mucous pouring out of our noses while trying to put on our gas masks. We wanted to break their despicable, low down, rotten necks. Ha! A year or so later I had to go through the tear gas chamber at Camp Lejeune during prison guard training. It was just as terrible the second time as it was the first time.

The combat rifle range target areas were the best part of infantry training school to me. Some courses had pop up targets and designated paths you traveled on in search of targets. Live fire training on those courses really fine-tuned us, especially if you loved shooting. I did pretty good on the ranges. I would have loved to be one of the instructors. At the machine gun course, I fired the M-60 machine gun. I shot the targets in half and was given extra training. I thought I might get a chance to be a machine gunner, but one of the instructors said they had their quota. I was an "0311-Infantryman" or what we called a "Grunt" and that would actually turn out to be very fortunate for me. The life expectancy of a machine gunner was a heck of a lot less than a grunt. The Lord works in mysterious ways!

We spent about five weeks at infantry training and were assigned our military occupational skills. As I said, I was made an 0311-infantryman. About ninety-five percent of us became grunts. We were now entering the backbone of the United States Marine Corps. We were not quite there yet, but we were getting close. Our new orders were sending us to Camp Pendleton, California for more advanced infantry training. They gave me a bus ticket to Birmingham, Alabama and a plane ticket from Birmingham to San Diego, California. I was given ten days leave/travel time, not charged out to my regular leave time, before I had to report to Camp Pendleton. Sweet! I couldn't wait to get home to see everyone and show off my new uniform. Pretty naïve, eh? Oorah! Marine Corps!

Needless to say, my leave time was wonderful. I could not get enough of all the great food that I had missed, and I tried to visit with everyone to catch up with all that had happened while I was gone. I was happy to see mom and dad back together again. The love and support of my family has always been fantastic, but they took it to an incredible new level when I was away from home in the Marines. I told them how much their letters and care packages meant to me and to please keep sending them to me. I tried not to show how nervous I was concerning how my life was about to change and no one really pressed me with awkward questions about it. My leave time just was not long enough, and the days flew by way too fast. It was hard to say good-bye to everyone, but I had to report to my next duty station. Mom drove me to the Birmingham, Alabama airport. On the way, we stopped by where my dad worked, and I said good bye to him and gave him a hug. He told me to be careful and that he loved me. When I got on the plane, it dawned on me that my dad had never told me that he loved me before. His words really made me feel good and I wished our relationship could have been different over the past years. His alcoholism ruined his ability to have a normal family relationship. Sadly, our good bye was the last time I saw him alive.

4

Camp Pendleton

My first airplane flight was nice. I had never thought about flying before. Seemed to me to be a great way to get somewhere fast. Now-a-days I could care less if I ever get on another plane. Go figure! The airport at San Diego was kind of confusing. With a little help, I made it to the bus stop. There were other Marines reporting in so that made it a little easier. We all unloaded at Camp Pendleton and were given a ride to where we had to report with our orders. It turned out to be about the same routine as Camp Geiger. We were assigned a barracks and met our instructors, a staff sergeant and a sergeant. One of the new things we were allowed to do was obtain temporary passes to go off base, usually to Oceanside, California. Also, we could eat at a mess hall, the enlisted men's club or buy food from a food truck that was allowed to come onto the base. It was pointed out that if we were not old enough, we could not drink alcoholic beverages on base nor off base. I had tasted beer and whiskey but had never had a whole beer nor alcoholic drink in my life, so who cared.

Our instructors were both Vietnam combat veterans that were about to be sent back to Vietnam for their second tour of duty. Our staff sergeant had a silver star and a Vietnamese Cross of Gallantry. Both of them had been wounded and awarded purple hearts. They were tough looking Marines and we were lucky to be able to learn from their combat experiences. Their knowledge about what we were about to face in Vietnam was real and they wanted us to be ready to meet the challenge. We were extremely lucky to be assigned to them and they explained to us that the next couple of weeks would be strenuous, both physically and mentally. They were exactly right about that. Thank goodness we were in good physical shape, because that helped us get through the next few weeks. At least we were able to get off-base passes during our free time. That helped our attitudes a bunch.

Our barracks area was about like what we had at Camp Geiger. We had wall lockers and foot lockers to stow away our uniforms and personal items. After we were able to get things organized, we formed up and were double timed over to the battalion armory where we were issued a M-14 rifle and all the "782" gear we would need during our training. We did not realize it, but the physical strenuous part had started. Everywhere we went was at double time pace and there was always time to climb the ropes at the rope towers, run the obstacle courses and it just would not be right if we did not do a couple of hundred pushups, sit-ups, chin-ups, thrusts and leg lifts.

The organized and un-organized runs were best described as "brutal." We always ran in formation. I do not think any of us thought that we could run more than we did in boot camp or at Camp Geiger, but we did. Running up hills and running down hills. Running with full packs and running with just our webbing with canteens. We always ran with our rifle no matter what combination our instructors wanted. Running down a steep hill with a rifle and full pack was about one of the hardest runs imaginable. A break in our instructor's mind was a run in our "T" shirts and gym shorts, without our rifles. They figured that since we were not encumbered with a rifle, pack or webbing we could run a little longer and further. Oorah! Marine Corps! Our instructors ran the same run we ran with the same gear. Talk about leading by example! We really respected those two instructors and we realized that they were getting themselves ready for Vietnam, too. They knew what we were about to face and wanted us ready by making us tough as nails.

Mixed in with the running and exercising were classes ranging from land navigation using a compass and maps to familiarizing ourselves with specific things we would soon be facing in Vietnam. We learned about mines and booby traps, now called I.E.D. for improvised explosive devices. The myriad ways the enemy could construct and place a mine or booby trap was amazing and it was an on-going learning curve. We were told that for every device we could detect and come up with a counter measure for, a new and improved device would show up. We learned that mines and booby traps encountered during combat patrols accounted for many Marine casualties. Little did I know that within ninety days I would be one of those casualties!

Another interesting class was the prisoner of war indoctrination class with an escape and evasion training exercise. We learned about the Geneva Convention, what to say and try to do if we were captured and how to treat prisoners. A mock prisoner of war camp was used for our escape and evasion exercise. The object was to get out of the camp and to safety without getting caught. No one made it to safety after they escaped the prisoner of war camp. Later, our instructors told us not to worry too much about the whole prison camp thing because as enlisted infantrymen we probably would not be captured anyway. The Viet Cong (V.C.) and the North Vietnamese Army (N.V.A.) usually did not want any live enlisted Marine infantrymen. They wanted officers or someone important. Ordinarily, the V.C. or N.V.A. just shot enlisted Marine infantrymen, used them for bayonet practice or had a little fun torturing them. They told us that we would not want any of them alive either, especially if we were moving through their positions during a fire fight. That really made us feel warm and fuzzy.

All in all, most of the classes reinforced what we had been taught in other classes and added to our growing knowledge base. We were starting to understand what we had to do as Marine infantrymen and when we needed to do it. I think all of us knew that nothing could really totally prepare us for combat in the short training time we had before we were actually in combat. It appeared to me that we would have our hands full just trying to stay alive long enough to learn how to survive in combat. There was probably much more we could learn and needed to learn, but our training time at Camp Pendleton wound down quickly and our orders sending us to Camp Smedley D. Butler, in Okinawa, were awaiting us.

I would be remiss if I did not talk about my off-base excursions while at Camp Pendleton. I was surprised how many of us had never smoked a cigarette, drank a beer or drank an alcoholic drink. Drugs were not even thought about, much less used and you thought of them as the bane of those crazy hippies. Most of us did not cuss when we went to boot camp, but we were starting to use a little more flowery speech, after all we were big, bad Marines. Oorah! Marine Corps! We figured that we might be dead in a couple of months, so we threw caution to the wind. It was really not a surprise that the first thing we would experiment with when we were given passes to go off base was drinking beer at whatever place we could get into without them worrying about our age. After all, we were big, bad Marines and had a reputation to uphold. Ha!

Most of us were only eighteen, but there were a few that were older. They would buy the beer and we would pay them back. It was a good deal for them, because they basically drank free beer at the expense of naivety. I think most of us did not care for the beer or mixed drinks. We felt it must be an acquired taste. The drinking led to carousing, because a surprising number of us were virgins and that pointed towards the clubs with naked dancers. We were really fascinated by what they wore and what they did not wear, not to mention the things they did. We received a crash course on the things we thought we had missed in life. I talked to the Lord pretty fervently about my transgressions then and later. Thank the Lord for his forgiveness and grace, not to mention the casting of our sins as far as the east is from the west. Sometimes, even the good Lord cannot help someone that is bound and determined to do something stupid.

Now I know stupidity will run a course through your mind and actions after a while, but me and my Marine buddies just could not leave stupid alone. I'm not talking about the drinking and carousing type of stupidity, nor the fighting and cussing type of stupidity. I am talking about having someone burn a USMC tattoo with a bulldog wearing a World War One helmet somewhere on your body or even brand a globe and anchor on one of your arm's type of stupidity. One night, while in Oceanside, California, we had been quaffing a few beers and came up with the bright idea of getting a USMC tattoo on our arms. We had noticed several tattoo parlors located on the same street as the bus stop where we caught our bus ride to the base, and we figured stopping by one of the tattoo parlors on the way back to the base was a really bright idea. I did mention we had quaffed a few brewskies, right?

Although I was a little nervous about the whole tattoo idea, herd mentality kicked in, along with the beers that were in my system, and I entered a tattoo parlor with the rest of my Marine buddies, bound and determined to get me a genuine USMC bulldog tattoo. Luckily for me, I was the last one in line and after smelling burned skin and hearing a couple of howls, old Jimmy just kind of eased out the door and caught the next bus to the base. I can still smell that flesh burning. It appeared to me that looking at a tattoo on my body for the rest of my life was not as appealing to me as I thought it would be. At the time, I did not know whether to be proud of myself or ashamed. Looking back, I'm glad I did not get a tattoo, but I really caught heck from my Marine buddies. The next morning, when all of us were in the showers, the tattoo recipients were complaining about how sore they were and asked me why I was not sore like them. I showed them my arms and they really gave me a ribbing about not getting a tattoo.

Fortunately for me, my time at Camp Pendleton was winding down quickly and my orders to Camp Butler were in my hands or old Jimmy might have been tempted to get that Marine bulldog tattoo in spite of myself. The devil was trying to find some weak spot on me to work on. Get back, devil! I never did get a Marine bulldog tattoo. I guess I was thinking more about jungle warfare training at Camp Smedley D. Butler, in Okinawa and what was going to happen to all of us in Vietnam than I was about a tattoo. As a matter of fact, I have never had the urge to get a tattoo since I was in training at Camp Pendleton. All of us were starting to realize we were getting closer and closer to earning our keep on the battle field. It was a very sobering moment for most of us. We were actually leaving the United States for the first time in our lives and going to a foreign land, fraught with all the dangers we had been training for.

5

Camp Butler

At the end of our training at Camp Pendleton, most of us received our orders sending us to Camp Smedley D. Butler, in Okinawa. Some were sent to various duties other than Vietnam. We flew to Okinawa on a commercial airline. From the airport we were bussed to Camp Butler. A sergeant formed us up, told us about our training schedule, marched us to our barracks and gave us some time to store our gear. When we had everything stored away, we were shown where the mess hall was located and told we had the rest of the day off. Everyone decided to get something to eat and walk around the base. The history of the World War II battle of Okinawa was well known to most of us and we were enthralled that we were actually on Okinawa. This was probably the first time any of us had been outside the mainland of the United States, much less been in a foreign land and on an island to boot! For all of us, we had experienced a lot of new things over the last few months.

Our jungle warfare training was oriented towards the conditions we were about to experience. A steady diet of running, exercising, climbing ropes at the rope towers and running obstacle courses kept our minds clear and our stamina up. Oorah! Marine! Corps! I do not think there is a Marine base anywhere that does not have rope towers and obstacle courses. There were a lot of classes about mines, booby traps and how to survive in combat. The classes and field training exercises were interesting. I do not know if that was because we were about to actually experience combat or if it was because we were starting to mature with the training a bit. We definitely paid more attention and had better attitudes than I had noticed in other training phases. Most of the instructors were really good and had served with infantry units in Vietnam. We were intent on learning everything we could from them to help prepare us for what was coming. I think we were starting to acknowledge the seriousness of what was about to happen to each of us. We even wondered if we ever see home again and if we did, would we be the same as we were before we left home. Talking about and training for combat in Vietnam is one thing, but the fact that we were now only days away from actual combat in Vietnam was something else. It affected everyone in different ways, but mostly we were just anxious to get it over with and wrapped our minds around it.

When training was over and we had received our orders to Vietnam, we were given instructions about what we would be allowed to take with us to Vietnam. It was not much, just toiletry items, extra socks, extra underwear, an extra set of utilities (green pants and shirt), an extra pair of garrison boots and a pair of shower flip flops. All of the items fit in a small, watertight utility bag. Later, I wondered why we took the extra pair of utilities, garrison boots and flip flops. The irony was not lost on me because one of the first things we did when we got to our battalion area was to turn our utilities and garrison boots in at the battalion supply depot where we were issued jungle utilities and jungle boots, along with other items we needed in the field. I never used nor do I know what happened to my shower flip flops. The sacrosanct wisdom of the United States Marine Corps is inviolate! There was a possibility that no jungle utilities nor jungle boots would be available for issue as all of us knew there were Marine barracks with concrete floors and showers all over Vietnam. Yeah, right! Every good Marine infantryman knows that he must wear flip flops while in the shower in Vietnam. Ha! Did I step through the mirror into Oz again?

We were not allowed to go off base while on Okinawa. We did get to go to the base enlisted men's club. I tried beer again, but still had not acquired a taste for it yet. We read books and played a lot of card games in the barracks to pass our free time away. Western books were the most popular reading material and hearts, or spades were the most popular card games. There was some gambling that went on in the form of poker and dice. I had never played poker nor rolled dice and I did not intend to lose what little money I had to a poker or dice shark. Most of the southern Marines did not play poker or roll dice. A lot of the northern and big city Marines did. Some of the things I was exposed to while in the Marines were really interesting and educational while some were better off forgotten. I guess Jimmy was truly exposed to Oz! Who would have ever known a tale like "Alice in Wonderland" could be so true in real life. I had learned a lot in a short time but knew I still had to apply what I had learned to the reality of Vietnam.

A captain talked to our training group after we were given our orders to Vietnam. He pointed out that failure on our part to report to our shipping out point would be tantamount to desertion, an offense that could have dire consequences. That gave us some food for thought because we had heard rumors that there had been instances where Marines had deserted to avoid going to Vietnam. The captain's talk reinforced the rumors. He told us that if we noticed anyone trying to desert, shirk their duties or feign sickness to get out of going to Vietnam, to find the sergeant of the guard and report the individual immediately. No one in our group missed our plane to Vietnam.

The night before I shipped out to Vietnam, I wrote a couple of letters to my family, went to the mess hall, walked around the base for a little while, stopped by the enlisted men's club, then headed back to the barracks to get cleaned up and hit the sack. My Marine buddy in the top bunk had been in boot camp with me. We played cards and quietly talked with some other Marines for a bit. The Marine with the first fire watch yelled out to wind down whatever we were doing as it was nearly time to turn out the lights. Everyone settled in for what we did not realize at the time was our last full night of sleep for a while. Thinking about what was about to happen to me the next day was not conducive to a good night's sleep.

Not long after the lights went out, I felt someone sit on my bed. I thought it was one of the Marines in the top bunks taking off his boots when I felt someone lay down on top of my blanket and start hunching me. I knocked him off my bed and grabbed a nearby helmet and started yelling at him while beating the living heck out of him with that helmet. The fire watch turned on the lights and alerted the sergeant of the guard who grabbed hold of me and told me to stop hitting the Marine. Fortunately for me, another Marine shouted out that the Marine that had crawled onto my bed was the same one that had tried to get in his bed the night before. I was sure glad he spoke up, because I did not want anyone getting thoughts about me being weird or something. I have often thought back to that night and wondered if that Marine was feigning homosexuality just to get out of going to Vietnam or out of the Marines. Looking back, I hope it worked for him.

The morning we were to be shipped out to Vietnam was a flurry of turning in equipment and packing all of our gear not going with us in our sea bags. We took our sea bags to the base overseas storage area, filled out the paper work and stored our sea bags until we returned from Vietnam. I did not know it at the time, but that was the last time I would see my sea bag and the items packed in it. There are many reasons why we did not get our sea bags back. They ranged from getting killed, wounded or downright thievery. I know I was wounded and never returned through Okinawa, but I did fill out the paperwork to have my sea bag sent to me. That was a waste of time and effort. Everyone I talked to that did not get their gear back, figured that some knuckleheaded "in the rear with the gear" jerk supplemented his pay by selling our stored gear on the local black market. R.E.M.F. (You can figure it out yourself!) was another name we called those "in the rear with the gear" knuckleheads that took advantage of us "Grunts." We tried to "square things away" with them every chance we got. Oh well, you know what they say: "Payback is hell!" I will probably never know why I did not get my sea bag back, but the repercussions of not having a complete U.S.M.C. clothing issue would later cause me unnecessary angst.

One of the sergeants shipping out with our group advised us to go to the mess hall and have a decent, hot meal before we went to the airport. He told us it would be the last, sit-down in a mess hall meal we would have for a while. I was not really hungry, but I am glad I took the time to eat. I figured the sergeant knew what he was talking about and as it turned out, he was right on target. Over the years, as I have thought back about my Vietnam experience, it was the little things that stuck out in my mind. Sometimes we take the little things in life for granted and do not realize how important they are until you miss them. The pleasure of a peaceful, quite meal is one of those things. During my time in Vietnam, the importance of many things I had taken for granted in my life would become apparent. Paramount among those things is that the Lord works in mysterious ways! Thank you, Lord!

6

Welcome to Vietnam

We flew to Vietnam on a commercial airliner and landed at the Da Nang military airfield. The air conditioning in the airliner was quite a contrast to the blast of humid, hot, stinky air that hit us when we went through the door of the airliner and down the steps to the airfield tarmac. Wow! Talk about a shock to the olfactory senses. Welcome to Vietnam! Commercial airliners, helicopters and military fixed wing planes were taking off, landing or parked in revetments. Concertina wire obstacles and sand bagged bunkers with armed guards were spaced at intervals around the airfield. Artillery and what looked like anti-aircraft batteries were placed behind stacked sandbag emplacements. A lot of hustle and bustle was going on everywhere around us.

The new arrival receiving area was pointed out to us and everyone went to the receiving area to turn in our orders. It took a while to sort everyone out and send them to their assignments. Some of the new arrivals already knew what to do and where to go or had transportation waiting on them. Most of us were told to go to a holding area and wait for transportation to our respective battalion areas. At the holding area, those of us that did not get transportation were formed up and sent to the first sergeant in charge of the perimeter for temporary duty assignments. We immediately realized we had been given the green weenie because some of the assignments were literally pretty crappy, as in cleaning out poop filled, cut in half fifty-five-gallon metal drums used at the latrines. We were instructed to pour diesel fuel in the drums, light the fuel and the contents of the drum on fire and to stir the burning contents occasionally with a hoe. Oorah! Marine Corps! When the first sergeant heard us grumbling amongst ourselves about the latrine detail, he reminded us that we were insignificant, low ranking, worthless newbie enlisted men and we would get over it. As he walked off laughing at us, I

I wanted to sling some burning poop at him with the hoe or possibly chop his head off with the hoe. Ha!

If you have never burned drums full of poop with diesel fuel and you are a depraved, inhuman, sadistic individual, then you need to go find a half fifty-five-gallon metal drum full of poop and burn it with diesel fuel. I have never met anyone that would volunteer to burn poop filled drums a second time in their life without a gun pointed at their head. The fumes and smells that emanate from the burning drums make your eyes water like you are crying and make you gag so violently that you throw up whatever you had eaten in the last twenty-four hours. Later, I was glad we had to turn our stateside clothing issue in and were issued our new jungle utilities, because we could not wash all of the stinking smell out of the stateside clothing. Everyone that would walk within one hundred yards of where we were working, would scurry as fast as they could to get on the "up wind" side of us, or they would try to down-right avoid us. I guarantee you that you will never forget the experience. It will stick with you for the rest of your life! I would still like to choke that stinking, pot-bellied, piece of poo first sergeant that assigned us to that duty, or at least get a chance to re-arrange his teeth. That was a really despicable assignment duty. Later on, after I had been wounded and I was a little more versed in how to avoid green weenie details, I would avoid checking in at the receiving area until the last moment and disappear from sight until my transportation arrived. Learning to avoid crap details in the Crotch became a sport for me and my Marine buddies.

After the poop burning experience, we were allowed to clean up at a nearby shower area. Believe me, when I say that all of us lucky new guys that got the green weenie poop burning detail really needed a bath after that humiliating experience. We were still retching while we were in the showers trying to wash the smell off of us and out of our clothes. The shower area was located inside a tent. When you took a shower, you would stand on a wooden pallet underneath a fifty-five-gallon metal drum full of cold water, pull on a wire or a rope attached to the lever of a spigot that was screwed into the bottom of the drum and water would drain out of the drum onto you. After you were wet and lathered up all over your body with soap, you would pull the lever and rinse off, trying not to use all the water in the drum. Occasionally, if you used all of the water in the drum, there was no more water available to put into the drum. That could be a bad situation if you had soap all over you and needed to rinse off! We lathered up our bodies with soap and rinsed off several times before we felt clean again. While we were bathing, we washed our uniforms and managed to get most of the crappy smell out of them. Thank goodness I got my unit assignment before that sorry piece of poo first sergeant could put me on another poop detail. The morning after the infamous poop detail, we were told our transportation was waiting on us outside the receiving entrance area. Hallelujah!

7

Golf Company, Second Battalion, Third Marines

I was assigned to Golf Company, Second Battalion, Third Marines (G-2/3) and was hoping that a helicopter would pick us up and transport us to our battalion area, but that did not happen. A couple of "six-by" trucks with fifty caliber machine guns mounted on the cabs of the truck, took us to our battalion area. We were issued M-16 rifles and ammunition with extra magazines at Da Nang. They gave us a crash course on how to maintain and use the M-16 rifle before we loaded up on the trucks. We had to turn the rifles, ammunition and magazines over to the truck crews when we got off the trucks. The sergeant in charge of our little "six-by" convoy sent us over to the battalion headquarters tent to turn in our orders and told us we would be issued rifles and other needed gear after we checked in at battalion headquarters. After we had turned in our orders and our personnel files, a corporal gave us some "C" rations, pointed out where we could get some drinking water and told us where to wait until someone called our name.

While we ate our "C" rations, we looked around the battalion area and noticed the battalion area was completely surrounded by a couple of rows of concertina wire with sandbag bunkers spaced around the perimeter. There were a couple of wooden towers, reinforced with sand bags, evenly spaced around the perimeter. All of the towers had machine guns and several of the bunkers had machine guns. It was pretty obvious that they had well thought out interlocking fields of fire. In addition, there were sand bag reinforced fox holes or fighting emplacements all around the perimeter. All of our company and platoon base camp areas would be set up basically in the same security pattern, only smaller and more primitive than the battalion area. We would soon learn that our company and platoon base camp areas would usually be the center of our assigned patrol areas.

Each base camp area usually had tents with sand bag walls around them or bunkers with sand bag reinforced roofs on them. Sometimes we could sleep on wooden and canvas folding cots, if they were available. Our rubber mattresses that we would be issued were usually put on top of the folding cots, when we got the chance to use them. I purposefully lost my rubber mattress as soon as I could. It was too hot to sleep on and too bulky to carry around. I never have liked to sleep on rubber or plastic. We slept on the ground while on patrol or in a fighting emplacement when we were at a base camp. We did not realize it at the time, but we would rarely get to use a folding cot, much less a base camp, except for a quick re-supply stop, or an overnight stop in between patrols. The immensity of all the things we were hearing and observing was really mind boggling to us. Just when we thought we had been trained to tackle anything and everything we were realizing that we had a lot to learn and a short time to learn it, if we wanted to survive.

A sergeant walked up to us as we were finishing our "C" rations with lists of names and unit assignments. He told us to look at the lists to see what units we were assigned to and then report to the supply sergeant for our "in country" field equipment issue. My individual unit assignment was the Third Fire Team, First Squad, First Platoon, G-2/3. We reported to the supply sergeant, turned in our state-side utility pants, shirt and garrison boots and signed the paper work for a pair of jungle boots, utility pants and utility shirt. The supply sergeant made us sign for our boots, clothing and other issue and informed us that we could not get another issue of clothing and boots unless we turned in what we had just signed for. At the time that sounded reasonable. Little did we know that the clothes we were issued would literally rot off of us because of the climate conditions, not to mention the accelerated clothing fabric wear-out due to combat patrol conditions in Vietnam. Plus, they usually cut your boots and clothes off you when you were wounded and med-evaced to a field hospital. Our jungle utilities just were not made to withstand the constant abuse associated with combat patrols in Vietnam. The inviolate wisdom of the Marine Corps could sometimes be puzzling. Oorah! Marine Corps!

Some of that wisdom was displayed at our next stop, the battalion armory. At the armory we signed the paper work for a M-16 rifle, magazines and "782" gear. At Da Nang we were issued M-16 rifles. We had turned them in to the sergeant in charge of our little "six-by" convoy when they dropped us off at our battalion area. I was relieved because to my knowledge, other than the crash course on how to use and maintain an M-16 rifle at the receiving area in Da Nang, I had never trained with nor fired an M-16 rifle. Not good! I thought it was a Mickey Mouse weapon compared to the M-14 or even the M-1 we used at Camp Geiger. The M-16 they issued us had a mechanical weakness associated with the ejection cycle. I think it had something to do with a weak spring. We learned to not fully load our magazines, to constantly clean our rifles as much as possible considering the extreme combat patrol conditions and to keep our cleaning rods or a stiff piece of wire handy in case you needed to push a round out of the chamber. At least I got my hands on a really good M-14 rifle at a later date.

Our "782" gear included a flak jacket, web belt, two canteens with mess gear, canteen covers, first aid gear and pouch, bayonet and sheath, grenade pouch, magazine pouches, field pack, "E" tool with cover, helmet, helmet liner and camouflage helmet cover, poncho, webbing straps, a blanket, a rubber mattress, a rubber lined utility bag and other assorted items. We spent a little time attaching everything that went on our web belt and field pack, loading our magazines with ammunition, putting our magazines in our magazine pouches placing everything we felt needed to go in our field pack and placing everything else in the rubber lined utility bag. A corporal told us not to sweat it because our individual squad leaders would square us away when we got to our units. Was he ever right!

Another small convoy of "six-by" trucks arrived to take us to our company base camp area. Our base camp and area of operations was south and south-west of Da Nang. The area we traveled through was mostly rice paddies, farm land, small villages, small coppices of trees and small streams. Interspaced within all of these features were small hills, while in the distance we could see larger hills and mountains. People were working in the rice paddies and farm land. We could see more people in the villages. Most of the traffic we encountered were military vehicles, civilian motor scooters, bicycles or people walking. Some of the people we saw were walking fast with a long bamboo pole over their shoulders. A basket or a bundle was attached to each end of the bamboo pole. They walked with a rhythm driven by the swinging of the baskets or bundles on each end of the bamboo pole.

Although they made it look easy, I would discover that carrying the weight they carried on those bamboo poles was not an easy thing to do. It was amazing watching them get under the bamboo pole, lifting the weight up while simultaneously swinging the load in a rhythmic motion not missing a beat. This would not be the first time I admired the strength, resourcefulness, fortitude or iron will of the Vietnamese people. I guess what really astonished me was the feeling that I had walked back in time, to a time without electricity, or many of the other modern necessities taken for granted back home. Wow! I was a long way away from Simmsville, Alabama. One more Oz moment, I suppose.

Before we left the battalion area the sergeant in charge of our convoy gave us instructions about how to mount and dismount the truck we were assigned to. Using the example of the numbers on a watch, he pointed out which direction around the truck each of us were responsible for such as one o'clock, two o'clock and so on. If we were ambushed and had to dismount, he pointed out our direction of fire based on the analogy of the watch. We were reminded repeatedly during the trip to our base camp to stay focused to the possible danger around us and to stay awake. The assistant driver was manning the fifty-caliber machine gun mounted to the cab of our truck. He was a continuous source of information about the Vietnamese people and the area we were traveling through, and he pointed out several areas where ambushes had taken place. We were receiving advice about paying attention to detail and if something did not look right, then it very well might not be right. We noticed that as he was talking, he never took his eyes off the surrounding areas we were traveling through. He emphasized that the one time you do not do your job or you do not pay attention is generally the time that you or one of your buddies will get killed or wounded. We traveled for a couple of hours before we could see a base camp in the distance. We could see and feel the drivers were getting nervous and one of our group asked the assistant driver what was up. He told us to shut up and pay careful attention to our surroundings, because just when you see your destination and you think you are safe, all hell can break loose. We shut up, looked and listened!

As we drove through the concertina wire, we felt like we had dodged our first bullet and I think all of us were relieved to dismount the truck. That euphoria did not last too long. We were hustled off to report to the acting company commander. Later, we would hear scuttlebutt about how several Marines were wounded and the most recent company commander killed by a mine that was triggered during a patrol. This had a very sobering effect on all of us newbies. Like all of those past instructors had told us, we had better listen up and pay attention. A thought had been nagging me since we left our battalion area. It finally dawned on me that there were quite a few of us newbies reporting in and I wondered what that was all about.

At the company commander's tent, we were told that a platoon leader or a squad leader would take us to our bivouac area. A group of grizzled Marines walked up staring at us. We newbies looked pretty clean and squared away, but there was something about these Marines that immediately sent signals to our newbie brains telling us to not smile, talk or do anything stupid. One of the Marines, a sergeant, started calling off names and told us that if we heard our name called, to fall in behind him. When he had called all the names we figured he was going to call, those of us that had heard our name called, walked over to where he was standing and fell in behind him. He looked at each of us and told us to follow him. The sergeant's name was Paul Reynolds. He was the bravest man I have ever met. He did not say much, but when he spoke, Marines listened. Sergeant Reynolds pointed out our squad bivouac areas and told us to report to our squad leader.

My squad leader's name was Sergeant Jim Bembry. He was a brave, experienced and knowledgeable squad leader that expected every squad member to pay attention to their surroundings and to do the job we were trained to do. That job was basically to close with and destroy the enemy. My fire team leader was a Private First-Class named Ronald Thompson. He was from Oklahoma and was one ornery rascal. Three of us reported to him. He immediately told us what equipment to get rid of and told us what gear and munitions we would need for the patrol we were going on in a few hours. Wow! For some reason I thought it would be a day or two before they cycled us into active patrolling. Welcome to G-2/3! I could not help but notice that nearly all of our squad were newbies like me. That nagging thought I had earlier about the large number of newbies reporting in led me to ask my squad leader why. He quickly informed me that I was a dumb a-- newbie! He said that everyone we were replacing had been killed or wounded and probably would not be coming back to our squad. I thought at that moment I would probably never see my family and Simmsville, Alabama again. Welcome to Vietnam!

All of the gear we were instructed to take on patrol, including a poncho, a first aid kit with pouch, a sharpened bayonet with sheath and a sharpened "E" tool with sheath, were placed in our packs or attached to our "782" gear. We placed loaded magazines in our magazine pouches and grenades in our grenade pouches. We filled our canteens with water. I used a half pack of root beer kool-aid in each of my canteens. It made the foul-tasting water taste better. A giant "Thank You" to my mom. She sent me packs of kool-aid in every letter and care package. We placed enough "C" rations for four days in our packs, along with extra socks, toilet items, a candle, writing material, "pop-up" flares and other assorted items. Some of us carried extra M-60 machine gun ammunition in a cloth shoulder harness, "claymore" mines, a "L.A.W." (light anti-tank weapon) and sometimes a mortar round attached to our packs. All of this gear, along with our flak jacket, helmet and rifle was an impressive sight of military hardware to behold, until you put it on your body. That was when you realized you were going to carry sixty to seventy pounds or more of gear while on patrol. Oorah! Marine Corps!

Carrying all the gear we had to have while on patrol was not without peril. Our flak jackets and other gear were cumbersome and chafed our skin. Everywhere the jacket or gear chafed our skin, jungle rot would infect the area. As a matter of fact, everywhere on your body where you cut or chafed your skin, jungle rot would infect that area. Jungle rot was a real nuisance, affecting practically everyone that fought and patrolled in Vietnam. We had to make sure everything was tied onto our packs and hooked into our webbing correctly to protect our skin from chafing, bruising or cuts. If something was not secured correctly it could affect our balance, possibly causing a fall or a pulled muscle. Everything needed to be tied down tightly or taped to keep the noise down. Noise discipline was imperative. We did not want to make it easy for Charlie (Viet Cong) to know where we were.

The heavy weapons munitions we carried were needed to support our M-60 machine gun and occasional mortar crew while on patrol. It was hard for them to carry their weapons with accoutrements, plus all the ammunition needed by themselves. Claymore mines were used to protect ourselves from infiltration of our perimeter, or while setting up an ambush site. About the only time we used our L.A.W. was to knock out a bunker or emplacement. We called it our bunker buster. We generally had small blocks of explosives (Composition B or what we called C-4) and caps with us. We used the C-4 to knock trees down when we needed a landing zone area for med-evac and supply choppers. Also, you could set a small piece of C-4 on fire and it would heat up your "C" rations or coffee fast.

All of the gear we carried supported us in the field or in the "bush" as we called it. The bush was basically everything outside the barbed wire perimeter of our base camp. It did not take long for us to figure out how to lighten the loads we carried on our bodies while on patrol. We watched the Marines that had been in Vietnam longer than us and learned from them. We called them "Salts." They would take advantage of us newbies until we caught on. As attrition whittled us down and time passed, we became the new salts and took advantage of the newbies. It could be a vicious cycle, until you learned. Some of us would swap different types of "C" rations that were heavy for lighter "C" rations. Some of the personal things that we did not absolutely need were left at our bivouac area. During a firefight, you learned to pass your M-60 ammunition or mortar rounds to the heavy weapons crews first and then your load would be lighter until a re-supply mission brought in more ammunition or you showed mercy on one of your buddies and helped him carry some of his load. Most of the time everyone tried to help each other out. Sharing a few pounds here or there made life a lot easier for everyone.

8

Combat Patrol

Thus, began our cycle of patrols, one after another, over and over, adnauseam. We called them "meat grinders" for a reason. Someone was usually wounded and sometimes killed during a patrol and sometimes more than one person. It was imperative to never let your guard down both personally and as a unit. We were in a constant state of alertness. There were "booby traps" everywhere and you had to really pay attention to where you stepped. An unexpected sniper shot could come out of nowhere or we could find ourselves engaged in a "firefight" without warning and we were always wary of ambushes. Our rate of attrition was astonishing. By the first time I was wounded in early January of 1968, we were approaching a twenty to thirty percent attrition rate.

Along with the brutal patrols, we had to get acclimatized to the overall debilitating nature of the climate in Vietnam. It assaulted our bodies in the form of a formidable humidity, extraordinary monsoon rains and unbelievable heat. In addition to the climate we had to deal with the different types of terrain in our patrol area. We waded through rice paddies or walked along rice paddy dikes. The paddies were fertilized with human waste and just down right stunk. The nasty, contaminated water infected our bodies as it infiltrated all of our open sores and scratches. Frequently, the Viet Cong or the North Vietnamese Army would randomly place "pungi sticks" under the rice paddy water that could impale an unsuspecting Marine. A human-feces coated pungi stick caused a nasty wound. Many times, a pungi stick wound could become infected, causing serious complications resulting in an amputation, or a life-threatening situation.

Patrolling in Vietnam's rice paddies, jungle and mountains combined with Vietnam's suffocating climate, exposed us to heat related injuries. If the patrols, the climate, the different types of terrain did not brutally wear us down, there was always the constant lack of sleep, poor diet, parasites, biting insects (especially mosquitoes), leeches and diseases such as malaria or some form of dysentery that continuously attacked our bodies. I have read that the typical grunt lost approximately twenty to twenty-five percent of their body mass or weight from the constant combat patrols and the harsh conditions encountered while in Vietnam. I know that I weighed around one hundred and fifty pounds when I arrived in Vietnam. The last time I was medically evacuated, I weighed around one hundred and thirty pounds or less. My worms and parasites that were dealt with at the U. S. Naval Hospital in Agana, Guam, probably weighed three or four pounds. Ha! Add all of that to the combat wounds, nicks, scrapes, jungle rot, bruises, contusions associated with combat patrols and you have a recipe for a seriously debilitated Jimmy! Even if we got a break from patrolling for a few hours rest at a base camp, the crotch would give us the old green weenie by letting us fill sandbags, build fighting emplacements, stand perimeter guard or some other routine job the R.E.M.F.s could have done while we actually got some rest. Just another day for a Marine grunt!

I guess it really did not matter, because we were on just as high of an alert status at a base camp as we were on patrol. There was no real safe and secure area in Vietnam! We could receive sniper fire, mortar fire or be attacked by the V.C. (Viet Cong, Victor Charles or Charlie) or N.V.A. (North Vietnamese Army) anywhere at any time. No one really wanted to hear any belly-aching about anything. Everyone felt things were bad enough without a bunch of grousing. When anyone would start complaining about anything, someone would usually say "Welcome to Vietnam!" At the time, believe it or not, I think some of us felt a bit more safe on patrol, where we had a chance to maneuver instead of having to hunker down and take all of the abuse from the R.E.M.F.s at a base camp and Charlie too. Looking back, I think the opposite was true. Interestingly, later on after I was out of the Marines, I met a business associate that had been a F4 fighter/bomber pilot in Vietnam at the same time as me. He made a comment about how he was glad that he piloted an aircraft and was not a grunt on the ground like I was. I told him that was funny because we had talked about how lucky we were to be grunts on the ground, able to maneuver and not having to worry about crashing or bailing out to who knows where. It is amazing what fifty years of hindsight can do to your thoughts on a subject like combat in Vietnam. Here we were talking about dangers that were unbelievable and yet we were talking about which danger was the worse. Go Figure!

Unless we were wounded and laid up in a hospital, we never got more than an hour, possibly two hours of restless sleep for months at a time whether we were on patrol in the bush or at a base camp. Our regular night time routine while on patrol, while waiting in ambush for the enemy or at a base camp, would be to buddy up with someone, sleep an hour and watch for movement for an hour over and over, adnauseam. You could not really sleep most of the time because of the constant state of alertness. If you made a mistake or missed something, you or someone could be killed or wounded. I think we resigned ourselves to the fact that while we were in Vietnam, we were not going to get much rest or sleep during our thirteen-month tour of duty and hopefully we could catch up on our sleep and get some rest when our thirteen-month tour of duty was over. Oh boy! Jimmy was so tired and sleepy when I got back home from Vietnam that I slept for nearly forty-eight hours straight…and I did not even stay my entire thirteen-month tour of duty! It took me months to get used to sleeping in a bed for eight hours or more. At first, I would sleep on the floor, getting up every now and then to check my perimeter. You never knew when old Victor Charles might pay you an unexpected visit. Old habits die hard!

My first patrol started when we walked, single file, through the concertina wire into what we called "Indian country" or "the bush." It was in late November, 1967. Happy Thanksgiving! Our squad leader had taken time before we "mounted up" to explain in detail our order of march. He told us that he expected us to maintain a constant state of alertness and to be ready to respond instantly to any contact with the enemy or encounter with mines or booby traps, pointing out that our lives depended on our vigilance. He pointed out that everyone gets nervous or experiences fear. He said the thing to do was to trust in your training, to not let your nerves get the better of you and to learn to control your fear, pointing out that for some it was easy, while others struggled. He ominously stated that a few patrols, booby traps or a fire fight will winnow it out of you one way or the other. Wow! He did not sugar coat anything. I do not know if our pre-patrol talk was the greatest pep-talk I have ever heard, but I do know that it got our attention. Old Jimmy was thinking that maybe that poop burning detail back at receiving was not too bad after all. Maybe I could get my military occupational skill changed to 03-poop burner! Ha! I knew that I possessed a couple of things that could help me make it through the tough times that were coming; my faith in the Lord, my sense of humor and my ornery streak. Thank you, Lord! I would need a heavy dose of all three of them before I got back home to Simmsville, Alabama.

After listening to our squad leader, a lot of thoughts and feelings were coursing through our minds and bodies as we left behind the relative safety of our base camp and walked through the concertina wire. To say I was excited and nervous at the same time would be an understatement. I learned quickly to just keep breathing and putting one foot in front of the other. Early on, I noticed a slight "tic" in my jaw. I was pretty sure it was a mixture of nervousness, anxiety and a conscious or possibly unconscious fear of the unknown. This was real, not a fantasy like when I was a boy playing with my brother and friends. When I think about Vietnam, I realize we exhibited a tremendous amount of courage and fortitude every time we walked through "the wire" to conduct a combat patrol or to engage the enemy. Our discipline enabled us to control our anxiety and fear of the unknown. After participating in several combat patrols, some might generalize or categorize a combat patrol as routine. Those of us that experienced combat patrols in Vietnam would probably argue there was nothing routine, mundane, simple nor ordinary about any combat patrol. All of them were dangerous and could become deadly in seconds! You simply could not let your guard down for a second. I can truthfully say that since leaving Vietnam in 1968, a day has not gone by that I have not thought about Vietnam. It was seared into my mind and body. I will probably be thinking about Vietnam in some way on the day that I die. It all started with that first patrol when we walked through the concertina into "the bush."

Individual, "fields of fire" were pointed out to each squad member based on our specific place within our fire team and position within the squad. The first man in file was called the "point man" and he was responsible not only for an overall view of what was before us and detection of booby traps, but also for a one-hundred and eighty-degree field of fire in front of us. Everyone else behind the point man alternated their fields of fire to the left or right of the file except for the last man in line. The last man in line was called "tail-end Charlie" because he was responsible for the overall view of what was behind us, ensuring no one crept up on us from the rear. He had a one-hundred and eighty-degree field of fire behind us. It was imperative that all fields of fire overlapped. The fields of fire for the point man and tail-end Charlie was greatly reduced when everyone was in their respective firing positions. Generally, the squad leader, radio man and corpsman were in the middle of the file along with any heavy weapons attached to the squad. That way the squad leader could direct specific fields of fire and place our heavy weapons accordingly. Normally, a heavy weapons platoon M-60 machine gun crew was attached to our squad while on patrol. We usually did not have a heavy weapons platoon mortar crew attached to the squad unless we were participating in some sort of special operation.

Our squad leader checked each of us to make sure our equipment was tied down tight and not making any noise as we walked. He reminded us to stay as quiet as possible with no talking as we passed through the concertina wire. We used hand signals and motions to direct attention where it was needed. Maintaining noise discipline was crucial and it was imperative to be on high alert while leaving or entering a base. Charlie knew we might relax or let our guard down leaving or entering a base camp, making the base camp vulnerable to an attack and our patrol an easier target to ambush. We learned quickly that we had to be painstakingly vigilant at all times to our surroundings or we could pay a blood price. I was always uneasy when we walked through the wire going on a patrol or coming back from a patrol. Most of the time I did not realize the perimeter of a base camp was out of site because I was so concentrated on detecting movement around us. We knew danger could be near and we could not afford to get comfortable in our routine while we patrolled. Some things, like radio frequencies and recognition codes, could change from one patrol to the next patrol. It was very important for us to memorize these things. We carried different colored "pop-up" flares or smoke grenades to be used as recognition signals. When we needed to enter a base camp, mark our position for helicopters or identify ourselves, we "popped" recognition flares or smoke grenades in the recognition signal order agreed upon before we started our patrol or as requested by helicopter pilots. A recognition signal order could be a red flare followed by a green flare then a yellow flare or in any other order planned, depending on the patrol orders. Not following prearranged recognition signal codes could cause a "friendly fire" incident where members of the same unit fire at each other. We generally avoided the risk of a friendly fire incident by hunkering down in a safe perimeter before we popped our recognition flares. Better to be safe than sorry!

Sometimes recognition codes could change while we were on patrol and we would have to break radio silence to confirm who we were. We tried to maintain radio silence while on patrol and only talked on the radio as necessary. In order to keep the radio chatter down, radio recognition codes were used while on patrol. We would press our radio handset to make a brief static noise to respond to a radio call. One brief press of the radio handset would produce a quick static sound. I still remember one call sign, or code, that was used on several of our patrols at specific time intervals; "Three Golf Alpha, Three Golf Alpha, this is One Golf Alpha." "If all is well, key your handset twice." We would generally key the radio handset twice indicating that we were alright. If we did not key our handset twice our platoon sergeant or platoon commander would know we were not receiving the radio signal, could not answer at that moment, might be in trouble or our batteries were used up. None of us griped about hauling an extra battery in our backpacks because we knew how important our radio was to us. While on patrol, in the middle of nowhere, our lives depended on the ability to use our radio. It was basically our only source of communication to the outside world. Without it, we could not call for help and that could be disastrous.

When we went through the wire, we usually melded into our surroundings quickly. It was kind of hard to do that if we were patrolling through rice paddies or villages. Sometimes, we would be in open terrain that looked fairly innocent and at other times we would be in areas so thick you could not see two feet in front of you. One thing we were sure of is that there was no such thing as a safe area or innocent looking situation while on patrol. You just never knew when all heck could break loose. Some areas were known for sniper activity or likely areas for ambushes, while other areas were known as "Indian country" where we would probably get in a firefight. Other areas were known for the numerous booby traps encountered. We frequently discovered weapons, food caches, tunnels, fighting positions and areas with prepared fields of fire. We filed all these little tidbits in the back of our minds because the ability of Charlie to work right under our noses was disconcerting. We tried not to travel down the same trail twice, because Charlie would leave us a few booby traps to contend with or lie in wait to ambush us occupying the same tunnels, firing positions and prepared fields of fire areas we had discovered weeks earlier. That is why it was important to file anything and everything you encountered while on patrol in the back of your mind. It might save you and your squad unnecessary casualties. Charlie and the

N.V.A. could be extremely dangerous if you did not stay on top of things while on patrol. They were very patient. Time was on their side. They were not going anywhere. This was their country, not ours.

We witnessed the incredible cruelty of Charlie and the N.V.A. regularly while on patrol. They wanted to let us know they were around and what they were capable of. The things we saw that the V.C. and N.V.A. did to Vietnamese villagers was unthinkable. The viciousness and barbarity of the things done do to the villagers to control them was like something from the worse horror movie you could imagine. I have wondered what someone could make me do if they raped and killed my wife in front of me, pointing out that if I did not do what they said to do, my sons and other family members would be tortured, suffering slow, painful deaths. I would have probably given in and done whatever was necessary to protect my family. Based on that, we could understand why someone could be chained to a tree and fire at us with an AK-47 rifle until they ran out of ammunition or was killed. Some of them really did not have a choice. I will never talk about the scenes of brutal atrocities Charlie or the N.V.A. perpetrated against villagers and left behind as an example for all to see. As we patrolled in and around some of these villages and observed these atrocities, they were seared into our minds forever. They are the terrible fodder nightmares are made of. I have read that infantrymen around the world, probably since the beginning of time, have always had a time-honored duty to protect those who cannot protect themselves. I know it was not our fault, but I have wished many times, over the years, that we could have been in a position to stop many of the atrocities suffered by Vietnamese villagers in our patrol area before they happened. Sadly, the poor Vietnamese villager suffered miserably from all sides during the fighting in Vietnam. Sometimes they were caught in the middle and did not have a chance to protect themselves. It would have been nice to get to know the Vietnamese villagers where we patrolled. It was just too dangerous for them and for us because of potential V.C. reprisals.

About the only time we got to visit with any Vietnamese was when we made an occasional stop at a small South Vietnamese Army (ARVN) base camp that was in our area of patrol southwest of Da Nang. The ARVN base camp encompassed the entire area of one of the odd hillocks that randomly popped out of the terrain in our patrol area. The hillocks were anomalies of the relatively flat terrain all around it. Most all of them were occupied, usually with a village built on and around them. I figured they built their villages near them or on them for the safety of the high ground during monsoon floods. We would usually spend a night at the ARVN base camp and continue our patrol the next day.   I wonder sometimes if some of the food offered to me by the ARVN soldiers at this camp introduced some of the parasites or the worms I had to deal with after I was med-evaced to Guam. The ARVN soldiers loved to play cards and get us to teach them how to speak English.   They tried to teach us how to speak Vietnamese. It was interesting. We would partner up with an ARVN soldier at night while on watch for enemy infiltrators. We were mortared a couple of times and occasionally received sniper fire while at that particular base camp.   I was impressed with the ARVN soldiers.   They were seasoned and tough.   Charlie was always attacking them, trying to wipe out their base camp, wounding or killing many of them.   I think they really appreciated us because our platoon had squads patrolling somewhere around them around the clock.   I never saw them leave their base and patrol like we did.   I do not know if that was intentional or they knew something we did not know.

Rarely did we get through a patrol without casualties.   My first patrol went through the wire with around fifteen Marines.   About four or five days later we returned to our base camp with twelve Marines.   The wounded Marines were victims of booby traps.   Charlie constructed booby traps in the areas we patrolled frequently or in areas they wanted to protect.   The types of booby traps could range from primitive hinged traps with many sharpened wooden spear-like projections to pungi sticks in holes or rice paddies.   Grenades of different manufacture or home-made mines made of old French or American ordnance were used in booby traps.   Manufactured mines of Russian and Soviet bloc countries were used frequently against us.

I was wounded the first time by a booby trap made with two American grenades in a hole with a trigger device made out of a wooden paddle that started out as a toy with a little rubber ball connected to a long rubber band attached to the paddle with a staple. I used to play with one of the doggone things, trying to bounce the ball off the paddle more times than anyone else could without missing the paddle.   We probably sent the toy to some Vietnamese child in a care package! Go figure! Fortunately for me, Charlie placed the grenades in a hole that was partially filled with water and mud. One of the grenades failed to completely detonate, while the mud and water absorbed a lot of the resulting blast and shrapnel. Thank you, Lord!

While on another patrol, two of my squad members were severely wounded, one of them losing his leg. The booby trap was a World War II era "Bouncing Betty" probably left behind or captured from the French when they were fighting in Vietnam. It was a gruesome scene. One of these guys (Wayne Thornton) saved my life a couple of times in fire fights and the other guy was our corpsman or "Doc" as we fondly called them. Doc had patched me up in the field several times and always had time to talk to us. Both of them were very special to all of us in my squad. That was a very sad and bloody day that has come back to haunt me in my dreams. I learned later that both of them survived. We found a lot of booby traps and mines on that particular day. When we set up a perimeter that night, we even found a booby trap made out of grenades in a water well within our perimeter. Fortunately, no one was wounded when it exploded, but it did kill a couple of chickens. The chickens were promptly cooked and eaten. Oorah! Marine Corps!

Mines and booby traps were Charlie's "go to" weapons in their fight against us. Charlie could make an explosive device or booby trap from pretty much any ordnance and masterfully conceal it. We really had to be observant. One time we patrolled in an area that B-52 bombers had carpet bombed. There were large craters everywhere. We observed a couple of craters with unexploded bombs. The bombs were huge. All of the unexploded bombs had been ingeniously booby trapped. Real courage was exhibited on Charlie's part to get in those craters and rig booby traps. I was impressed by their zealous, dogged determination in their fight against us. Personally, I never wanted to get any closer to unexploded ordinance than I had to. The number of mines and booby traps found depended on the area you were patrolling. If the N.V.A. were actively operating in your area of patrol, the number of booby traps encountered dropped drastically. The N.V.A. usually maneuvered in larger groups over wider areas than the V.C. and they did not want to fight us in areas where their maneuvers could be perilous to them because of their own mines or booby traps. Even then, we had to maintain our vigilance because the N.V.A. deployed booby traps for defensive purposes. Usually they were mines manufactured in Russian or a Soviet bloc country.

I got lucky with the first manufactured type mine I encountered. I was walking point, looking carefully around me, when I noticed a piece of cloth where I did not think it should be. One thing I had learned quickly while on patrol, was if something did not look right or looked out of place, I stopped immediately and held up a balled fist to signal everyone to stop in place and beware. After stopping, I carefully looked around and noticed disturbed soil in the path we were walking on. Closer inspection revealed some wire prongs sticking out above the soil. I placed a small piece of card board next to the mine and pointed it out to the next man in line and he relayed the information to the next man behind him and so on. Extreme vigilance was mandatory for a point man while on patrol. My experience walking point conditioned me to look for anomalies like that piece of cloth and the soil disturbance that I had noticed. Casualties were prevented on that occasion because I was paying attention to detail. Thank you, Lord!

Of all the things encountered while on patrol in Vietnam, mines and booby traps probably got my attention the most. Fortunately, we found most of them before someone was injured, but the mines and booby traps we did not see or missed, really caused a lot of casualties and heartaches. Most mines and booby traps usually maimed their unfortunate victims causing terrible wounds that would not only knock out the individual or individuals affected but would take the squad out of an offensive posture, placing it into a defensive posture. That was very advantageous to Charlie if he was attacking us or if he was trying to leave the area. Mines and booby traps encountered in Vietnam wounded or killed a lot of good Marines and left a gruesome legacy of amputations, broken hearts, scars and mental anguish. It has been fifty years since I was med-evaced from Vietnam and if there is one thing that has haunted me more than any other thing that happened while I was on patrol in Vietnam, it is probably the bloody scenes of carnage inflicted by mines and booby traps to me and the Marines I served with.

Unfortunately, mines and booby traps were not the only things we had to deal with while on patrol. Occasionally, while on patrol, we could suddenly find ourselves receiving rifle or machine gun fire from entrenched V.C. or a sniper. Most of the time the sniper was holed up in a well camouflaged fighting emplacement making it hard to locate and destroy. Charlie could dig a simple hole just big enough for one man and camouflage it with grass, leaves, twigs or whatever it took to blend the fighting position with the surrounding terrain. He usually made a cover for the hole that was so well camouflaged that we would nearly step on it before we discovered it. We called them "spider traps" because they could pop out of the hole, fire at us and disappear back into the hole in a heart-beat. Often, we encountered a series of fighting positions, reinforced with timber or set back in the tree line or along the trail just out of sight, but with a good field of fire. When we discovered them unoccupied, we would destroy them with explosives. If we could not destroy them, we would mark them on our maps and make a mental note of their location for future patrols in the area. Occasionally, these type fighting positions had V.C. waiting in ambush for us to get close to them. The resulting firefight could be brief or turn into an extended battle. Sometimes it seemed like we were only fighting for seconds and other times it felt like an eternity. Any way it happened, it felt like time stood still and at the same time all hell had been turned loose.

The violence and noise associated with a firefight is unbelievable. The sonic pop of a rifle round passing within inches of your head is something you will never forget. The lazy flight of a grenade sailing through the air right at you really got you moving, if possible. Otherwise you hunkered down, getting as small as possible or hoping you had enough structure of some type between you and the grenade's blast cone full of shrapnel. I still have a lot of grenade fragments all over my body. They look like little black freckles. The amazing thing experienced most of the time, is not realizing you were hit while other times you felt it burning or hurting immediately. I guess it was the adrenalin flowing through your body, brought on by the heightened nerve reactions responding to the tumultuous fury going on around you. During a firefight, you had to maintain situational awareness or die. If you did not pay attention, with your weapons ready to fire, Charlie could easily sneak up on you and your unsuspecting squad members and wreak havoc. I do not know if everyone "froze up" at one time or another during a firefight, but I do know that I briefly froze up for a few seconds on one occasion before I snapped out of it and started firing my rifle. I guess I just was not as prepared as I thought I was for those first few shocking seconds of my first firefight, but fortunately my training "kicked in" pretty quick. Involvement in an actual firefight is not child's play nor is it training, it is real, and it is extreme violence. I would not wish it on anyone.

I was wounded the first time in early January, 1968. Not long after I was med-evaced, my squad was involved in a terrible, deadly firefight. It was in an area that had sketchy artillery coverage and Charlie was aware of it. We had patrolled in and around the general area of the firefight several times before I was wounded. While on a routine patrol, my squad suddenly encountered a large group of V.C. and N.V.A. and was quickly involved in a firefight that nearly annihilated them. Six or seven were killed and several were wounded. It was only the heroic actions of a few that saved the squad members that survived. I was told that despite wounds to his jaw and neck, Sergeant Bembry was able to use the radio to call for support and arrange for the survivors to be med-evaced. One squad member was discovered alive within the enemy positions during recovery efforts. He had been shot and had fallen in a hole. Scuttlebutt was that he saved himself by covering himself up with nearby brush and debris. It was said that Charlie did terrible things to the bodies of some of the dead Marines that could not be immediately reached. The intense fire power directed against the surviving members of the squad prevented the immediate recovery of some casualties. Aggressive patrolling by Marine infantry units in Vietnam made these sudden, deadly encounters with the enemy a common occurrence. Even though I was in a hospital at the time, I actually suffered from "survivor's guilt" because I was not with my squad when they needed me that day. Survivor's guilt manifests itself in a weird way. The conundrum you find yourself in is that part of you feels guilty that you were not there while another part of you is glad that you were not. Sounds strange, doesn't it?

Strange things happened during some of the firefights I was involved in. I had a couple of flak jackets shot or blown off me. Both times I thought I had been hit hard only to discover no wounds or a couple of minor shrapnel wounds. Unbelievable! My pack had a few holes in it that were not in it before one fire fight and a couple of times my "782" gear took shrapnel hits without any damage to me. Go figure! My helmet was "dinged" a couple of times nearly tearing off my camouflaged cover, plus on occasion there would be several holes in my jungle jacket and trousers that I had not noticed before a firefight. Whew! Close calls. One of the most amazing things was when Sergeant Reynolds had us advance "on line" across a rice paddy while under intermittent fire and we did not take a casualty. If I were a betting man, I would have bet that several of us would have been killed or wounded. During one "hot" firefight I was involved in, Sergeant Reynolds calmly walked around pointing out fields of fire to us while we were down in fighting positions. I remember looking at him in amazement. He did not even appear to be nervous! I think we would have probably followed him to hell to fight the devil! He is one of the bravest men I have ever known. His leadership while under fire inspired all of us and none of us wanted to disappoint him.

On one platoon sized patrol, we were conducting search and destroy operations around select villages within our patrol area specifically looking for weapon and food caches. Sometimes it appeared that some villages supported Charlie more than others, not to mention the fact that we encountered more mines and booby traps around some villages more than others. These were the particular villages that we wanted to closely inspect for caches. While checking out one of these villages, we encountered sniper fire. We immediately returned fire at the muzzle blast we observed coming from one of the hooches within the village and started maneuvering ourselves towards the village. I had been temporarily assigned as a grenadier and was using a M-79 grenade launcher because our last grenadier had been wounded and med-evaced to a field hospital. We called the M-79 grenade launcher a "Blooper." I launched a couple of rounds into the hooch while a couple of Marines enveloped the sniper's position and killed him with rifle fire. The marine that killed the sniper came back waving his trophy AK-47 rifle over his head. After the brief firefight with the sniper, we found a cache of weapons and food. At another nearby village in search of weapons and food caches, a Marine named Greer stepped on a booby trap, wounding him. I think he was from Georgia. He had not been with us very long. Vietnam was a very unforgiving and frustrating place.

In early February, 1968 we were ordered to conduct a search and destroy operation around a village where some V.C. had been observed building fighting emplacements. Amtracks carried us from our base camp to a drop off point near the village, dropping us off alongside a large rice paddy. Amtracks are amphibious tracked vehicles used to carry infantry into combat behind the relative safety of their armor. They were capable of operating in water or on land. We nicknamed the amtracks iron coffins because they drew rocket propelled grenades like bees to honey. You did not want to be inside one of them when they ran over a mine or when they were hit by a rocket propelled grenade. I noticed that after the amtracks dropped us off, they formed up in a defensive position behind us. A M-60 tank, equipped with a flame thrower instead of an artillery tube, accompanied the amtracks to the drop off point. It stayed with the amtracks. We advanced across the rice paddy toward what looked like an elevated field with a tree line just beyond the field. When we emerged from the rice paddy onto the higher ground, we discovered ourselves in a group of open garden areas covered with furrows and lines of trees around the perimeters of the gardens. Little did I know that a couple of those furrows would save me from receiving serious injuries from grenades and rifle fire.

Nothing happened until we started advancing towards the tree line around the village. A machine gun opened up right in front of me and how he missed me I will never know. I heard the sonic pop of rounds passing close to my head and felt rounds popping all around me, but none hit me. Thank you Lord! After I dropped to the ground, I looked towards the noise created by the machine gun fire and could see the muzzle blast and a barrel sticking out of a well camouflaged spider trap. I started firing at the barrel and the area around the muzzle blast while another Marine killed the V.C. in the spider trap with rifle fire and a grenade. As I was about to get up and move toward what protection the nearby tree line offered, I heard a clash of gears and a motor revving up. I had been concentrating so hard on shooting into the spider trap at the machine gun that I never heard the flame thrower tank moving up behind me. It nearly ran over me. I shouted and rolled out of the way, towards the tree line and directed my fire towards the tree line where most of the V.C. fire was coming from. Sergeant Reynolds walked up to where my fire team was and pointed to us, indicating that he wanted us to place our casualties onto the tank and crawl up on the tank to provide covering fire against any V.C. trying to disable the tank.

I figured we would drop off our casualties where the amtracks had taken up a defensive position and rejoin the fight, but the tank proceeded toward the village. When the tank stopped about fifty feet from the tree line near the village, we figured it was going to burn up the tree line along with any defensive positions within the tree line. Before it could do anything, rocket propelled grenades (RPGs) shot out of the tree line and at least one hit the tank near where I had positioned myself on it. One of us must of hit one of the V.C. that was shooting at us with the RPGs, because one of the RPGs missed the tank completely. I do not know to this day whether I realized that one of the RPGs had missed while I was still on the tank or while I was flying through the air away from the tank. I do know that I was blown through the air about twenty feet away from the tank and towards the tree line hitting the ground hard enough to dislocate my shoulder and knock me unconscious.

When I regained consciousness, there was a dead V.C. laying across my legs staring at me. I fired a couple of rounds into him, luckily not hitting myself. Thank you, Lord! I heard Wayne Thornton yelling; "Kit, he's dead, watch out in front of you!" When I looked up, I could see vegetation moving and realized it was muzzle blasts of weapons firing at us. I returned fire and noticed a couple of black objects flying through the air towards me. It took me a second to realize they were grenades and it looked like they were going to land right on top of me. I pressed myself as far into the ground as it would let me and hoped that I had made myself small enough that I might escape the worst of the grenade's blast cone radius. They exploded right next to me and I figured I was a goner. Fortunately, when I was blown off the tank, I had landed between two furrows in a garden area. My shoulder hurt pretty bad but I did not feel any pain from the grenade shrapnel. Have I mentioned "Thank You, Lord" too much? I do not think so! Thank you, Lord! I started firing again only stopping when I noticed the firing in front of me had died down quite a bit. It seemed to me that we had been fighting all day long but in reality, it had only been an hour or two!

When I took inventory of my body and things around me, I noticed that I was bleeding from several places, plus my shoulder was not only hurting but it did not appear to be in its proper position. I also noticed that part of my flak jacket was missing, the stock of my rifle was damaged, my camouflage helmet cover was hanging down over the side of my face, my helmet had a couple of dents in it and that doggone V.C. had half of an old fashioned ice tong in his hand with the point sticking in part of my flak jacket. I felt a shudder go from the top of my head to my toes, because it suddenly occurred to me that if my fellow Marine fire team member had not shot this fellow, I might be a prisoner or the lead character in the torture games the V.C. probably had planned for entertainment that night. He had been about to drag me back to their defensive position with that ice tong while I was knocked out cold. That was a really close call. Thank you, Lord! Later, we linked up with the rest of the platoon and they med-evaced me to a field hospital near Cam Rahn Bay. Sergeant Reynolds told me many years later at a battalion reunion, that they found nearly a dozen dead V.C. in the tree line in front of us. I told him that Wayne Thornton was probably responsible for most of the dead V.C. they

found.   He is one heck of a Marine.   I am glad he fought next to me that day.
Thank you, Wayne!

After a couple of days in the field hospital, I returned to my unit with orders
to take it easy for a week or two.   Yeah, right!   That's a green weenie waiting
to happen.   As a result of the intense fighting brought about by the N.V.A.
and Charlie's Tet New Year, 1968 offensive, it was basically "all hand's on
deck."   I could not stay at the base camp and let my squad down, so I told
Sergeant Reynolds I was ready to rejoin my squad.   You would think I was
smart enough to know not to volunteer for anything, but like I mentioned
earlier about the tattoo escapade, stupid runs deep sometimes.   We went out
on patrol that night.   This would be the second time I went back on patrol
with stitches in me.   Doc's good care in the field while on patrol, combined
with all of the antibiotics they pumped into me at the field hospital probably
kept infection at bay until my body healed up.   Miraculously, I never had any
problems with infections other than the annoying "jungle rot" all of us seemed
to get at one time or another.   We did not get in any really bad firefights after
I rejoined my squad, but we were in the bush continuously on patrol and took
several casualties from booby traps, snipers and some brief firefights.

About a month after I rejoined my squad, we entered our base camp amidst
the hustle and bustle of loading up of our gear onto six-by trucks for a move
to a new area of operations.   Scuttlebutt had it that we were heading for an
area to reinforce the Fourth Marines.   They were operating in a mountainous
area northwest of Da Nang and were engaged pretty heavily with N.V.A.
regulars.   Scuttlebutt indicated that the Fourth Marines needed a breather and
a chance to regroup.   We figured we were in for it because the only time they
hauled us somewhere in vehicles or on helicopters, was when all heck was
about to break loose.   One sidebar for me was a chance to fire the fifty-caliber
machine gun mounted on the six-by truck I was assigned to.   I was asked to
test fire the fifty at a tree line.   Wow!   That was some fire power.   I was
amazed at the range and how the rounds impacted in the tree line.   If Charlie
was hiding in that tree line and watching us, he definitely sought cover.   That
was the only time I ever fired a fifty-caliber machine gun.   The six-by trucks
dropped us off and we patrolled towards an old, dilapidated, abandoned
French camp overlooking a valley with an abandoned railroad bed running the
length of the valley as far as you could see.   We were told that we would set
up a defensive perimeter at the old camp for the night.

I will remember the start of this operation until the day I die. We received some sniper fire and discovered several mines and booby traps while in route to the camp. While setting up defensive positions at the old French camp, we were told to stay alert because of the N.V.A. activity around us. All of us knew that it was going to be a tense, long night. Listening posts were set up around the perimeter to give everyone within the perimeter as much early warning of imminent danger as possible. A couple of us out of my squad were chosen for listening post duty about fifty yards away from our perimeter. One of us would try to sleep while the other would listen and watch. Around midnight, something let out an unreal, heart stopping scream that made both of us tighten up with our weapons ready to fire and just plain scared the bejeebers out of us. One of the mortar crews or someone popped a flare. In the false light of the flares, we saw a couple of faces. We were ready to start firing when it dawned on us they were monkeys. We did not sleep a wink after that stressful moment. We heard rifle fire, but the best we could determine it was probably directed at those monkeys. I hated listening post duty. It was very stressing, and you had to really stay alert not only for your own safety, but to make sure you gave as much early warning as you could to those in the perimeter of imminent danger. We usually had an escape route and prearranged signals established before we left the perimeter to set up a listening post. Occasionally, we would position claymore mines in a defensive posture to cover our retreat from the listening post back to the perimeter. Those claymore mines really packed a punch and you did not want to be in their blast cone radius when they were triggered. You did not want to be directly behind a claymore mine either, as the back blast could do some damage to you if you were too close to it.

The next morning, the company was assembled and lined out for a combat patrol that would follow the abandoned railroad bed and conduct a search and destroy operation of the surrounding area. We found several mines and booby traps that day. It was on that old abandoned railroad bed that we lost two men to the old, World War II era French bouncing betty. I described the scene earlier when I was discussing mines and booby traps. One of our beloved "Docs" and Wayne Thornton were wounded. I mentioned the grenade booby trap in the well that ended the lives of several chickens but livened up our fare at supper that night. We lost several Marines on this operation to mines, booby traps and firefights. After we left the abandoned railroad bed behind us, we slowly patrolled higher and higher into the mountains that surrounded the valley where the abandoned railroad bed was. The climb, at times, was tortuous and at other times we carefully followed a pretty well-worn trail. All of us knew that a well-worn trail indicated heavy N.V.A. traffic and possible mines, booby traps or ambushes.

While on this operation, I started experiencing pain and swelling in my left leg and knee. My right shoulder ached all the time. My left knee would collapse unexpectedly, and my left leg and knee just did not feel right. Doc kept me supplied with aspirin when I needed them for pain and ace bandages to wrap around my leg and knee for the swelling. He told me the pain and swelling were probably associated with my recent wounds, indicating a bigger problem that might have to be addressed in the future. He said that he would check on me now and then to see if the pain and swelling were getting worse. I told myself to "suck it up" and do my job, but sometimes the pain really bothered me.

Sergeant Reynolds sought me out while we were in a defensive perimeter for the night and told me I would lead a squad size patrol the next day. Part of me was honored that he would entrust a squad to my leadership while another part of me was a nervous wreck. I did not want to let Sergeant Reynolds down by getting good Marines wounded or killed. He explained what he wanted me to do and how he wanted it done, showing me the map co-ordinates of the patrol area and call signs. He said he would not have recommended me to the lieutenant if he did not have full confidence in my abilities. He had a way of making you feel worthy and I was proud to serve with him. I went back to my squad and started squaring them away in preparation for our patrol, ensuring that we had everything we needed.

Before daylight we walked through our perimeter and started our patrol. At intervals I checked in as ordered. My first patrol went off without a hitch and got easier as time passed. I kept my nerves in check but had to laugh at myself when my radio operator said my jaw kept moving up and down without me talking. I had noticed a "tic" in my jaw on my first patrol and figured it was just my body's response to stress. Firefights produced the same "tic" in my jaw. When night time came, I was ordered to set up an ambush alongside the trail the rest of the company would be traversing the next day. We set up a perimeter and after nightfall moved to the first prearranged ambush site. We noticed no movement and after about four hours, moved to another prearranged ambush site, hoping no N.V.A. heard us. Nothing of any interest happened and we waited until we saw our platoon on the trail and rejoined them. I must say that I was relieved we did not engage the enemy and made it back to our platoon with no casualties. Thank you, Lord! I was proud that Sergeant Reynolds had faith in me and my abilities. He saw something in me that I did not know was there. Even though I was only a temporary squad leader, until a more qualified replacement joined our ranks, the experience was a real leadership eye opener that has been invaluable throughout my life.

Not long after we rejoined our platoon, we got into a firefight with some N.V.A. in entrenched positions, killing several of them, but we had casualties also. The N.V.A. positions had been well made and positioned in such a manner that we were nearly on top of them before they opened fire on us. We left the N.V.A. bodies where they fell. If any more N.V.A. were around, they chose not to engage us. We found numerous holes with camouflaged covers and established, interlocking fields of fire. There must have been more N.V.A. around at one time or another. A landing zone was cleared, and our wounded were med-evaced. Later, as I walked around the area of the fire fight, I noticed more unexploded blooper rounds than I had ever seen. I do not know why they did not explode and warned my squad to avoid them just in case they were capable of exploding. After our wounded were med-evaced, we continued our patrols in the mountains for another week or so, ending up in the valley with the abandoned railroad bed, only further north from where we originally started. There were a few more casualties from mines, booby traps and firefights. I think everyone was ready to move on out of those mountains to a new patrol area. We were loaded up on six-by trucks and trucked to an air base somewhere north of Da Nang near Phu Bai where our company had set up a bivouac area. I ate my only mess hall prepared meal that I had while I was in Vietnam at that air base. They prepared an excellent meal for us and we were allowed to eat all we wanted. It was really good.

We found out why we were treated so well the next day. Our battalion was starting a new operation within forty-eight hours. The scuttlebutt was that we were going up near Que and work our way north and west to help the Ninth Marines at Khe Sahn. They wanted us rested up a bit and well fed for the slaughter. Ha! We were issued new jungle utilities, underwear, socks and even got to take a shower under a fifty-five-gallon drum set up with a shower head. A bunch of newbies arrived to replace our losses and my squad got a new squad leader. I was no longer the temporary squad leader and was relieved that I was a fire team leader again but was aware that combat attrition changed those type things quickly. I was learning to enjoy what little down time we were afforded in combat and tried to stay out of sight. If the R.E.M.F.s could not see you, they could not put you on a work detail doing chores that they should be doing anyway. If you were smart, you learned how to avoid most of the green weenie details. One thing we could not get out of was perimeter guard duty. I stood perimeter guard a couple of times while we were in our bivouac area. The short break helped my knee and shoulder issues, although I was still experiencing some pain. The start-off point for our new operation was in an area that we had not patrolled in before. The terrain was flat and sandy. Luckily for us, it had rained pretty hard the night before we started the operation. The rain had exposed many booby traps for us. Most of them were pungi stick booby traps, but some were rigged with explosives. Charlie had used dark plastic to cover the holes and had sprinkled sand over them to camouflage them. Thank you, Lord for the heavy rains that washed the sand off the plastic! There were casualties from mines and booby traps that day, but it could have been a lot worse. What little intermittent fire we received throughout the day caused some delays, but no casualties. We set up our defensive perimeter that night and I got to look through a star light scope a couple of times during the night. It was amazing what detail you could see through the scope. Scuttlebutt was that a couple of V.C. infiltrators (sappers) were seen and eliminated with the help of the star light scopes.

Our operation orders were to conduct search and destroy missions along with sweeps of enemy held villages and to find and destroy weapon and supply caches. Several V.C. and N.V.A. were killed during the operation. My left leg and knee started causing me problems during the operation and my right shoulder was constantly aching. Several times while running or jumping across a ditch my leg would just collapse, causing me to fall down. It was starting to get not only aggravating but posed a risk to my squad if it collapsed at a critical time. After a firefight, one of our Navy corpsmen noticed me limping pretty badly and grimacing from the pain. Doc asked me if I was alright and I told him my leg was really messing with me. He checked me out and noticed that my knee was badly swollen and that I was bleeding from some of my wounds. Doc placed a med-evac tag on me and told me to get on the med-evac chopper. I threw all of my gear to my squad members as the Huey med-evac chopper lifted off the ground. While the chopper was lifting off the ground, it occurred to me that my Vietnam combat patrolling days might be over. I did not know what to think about that as the chopper was flying me to the field hospital. The thought hit me that I had been med-evaced on a Sikorsky H-34 helicopter with eyeballs painted on both sides of the front of it, a Ch-47 (Chinook) helicopter that looked too awkward to fly and now on a Bell UH-1 (Huey) helicopter that looked like a thoroughbred war machine. Why I was thinking about the types of helicopters I had been med-evaced on was a mystery to me. Tears were running down my face as I watched the faces of my squad members disappear in the distance. A lot had happened to me in a short time. I thought back to the day in late November, 1967 when I stepped off that plane at the Da Nang airfield. Who would have guessed I could possibly be leaving Vietnam in May, 1968? My tour of duty was not supposed to be over until January, 1969. I had been in Viet Nam less than six months! For a while, I figured that I would never see Simmsville, Alabama again and now I realized I might make it back to Simmsville alive! Thank you, Lord!

The weird thing about it was I thought that I might be a coward for being glad I was finally out of combat. I knew that I was your average 0311 Marine "grunt" and was as proud as any Marine that has ever earned the right to wear the globe and anchor. With every step we took while on patrol and every firefight we fought in, we showed our fortitude and courage. Our blood was shed, parts of us were left on the battlefield and many fell, never to see what their future would bring. Purple hearts, medals and ribbons tell our stories to other warriors. We represented the cannon fodder fed into the daily squad sized "meat grinder" patrols, that become the standard by which all Vietnam Marine infantrymen will be remembered. Just as we learned from the Marine infantrymen that fought before us, the Marine infantrymen that followed us learned from us. Those Marine infantrymen passed their lessons learned to the Marine infantryman that followed them and the tradition continues. Semper Fi, Marines!

I told myself that I had not shirked my duty, that I had bravely walked every patrol and that I had courageously fought as hard as I could in every firefight I was involved in. What really made my Vietnam experience surreal, is that when I was med-evaced the last time, my squad's attrition rate was over 100%.

Imagine that! That means that every Marine in my squad when I joined it and several Marines that joined my squad after me, were either W.I.A. (wounded in action) or K.I.A. (killed in action). I do not know of one individual in my squad that left Vietnam unscathed. In 2010, at a battalion reunion in Tybee, Georgia, Paul Reynolds told me that the attrition rate may have been even higher than what I thought it was. Amazing! I had survived and had every reason to be happy. I would be able to go home to Simmsville, Alabama with my head held high. Still, for some reason, I felt like I was deserting my squad when I got on that med-evac chopper for the last time. Some say that survivor's guilt is not real, but on that med-evac flight to the field hospital, it was real and it was really playing mind games with me.

Alan Beasley, my minister at the First United Methodist Church in Jasper, Alabama, said in one of his sermons that God will help us navigate those areas in our life where fear reigns. He is so right. The second time that I was wounded, a Catholic priest basically told me the same thing. While in route to the Cam Rahn Bay Field Hospital on that med-evac chopper, I prayed a prayer of gratitude and thankfulness for God's protection and mercy. By the time we landed at the field hospital landing zone, the Lord had helped me sort things out in my mind and I was at peace with myself. I needed to concentrate on getting healed and not worry about things I had no control over. The realization of what I had been through, how I had conducted myself and my irrational fear that I was letting my squad down would trouble me for a long time, but for the time being I needed to put those kind of thoughts on hold. It appeared that Jimmy was headed for a long hospital stay, but before I write about my long recovery, I need to take some time and write about med-evac choppers, field hospitals, the Hospital Ship U.S.S Repose and the U. S. Naval hospital at Agana, Guam.

Vietnam
(Holding an M-14 with bipod)

9

Field Hospitals and The U.S.S. Repose Hospital Ship

The pilots and crews of med-evac choppers we called in to med-evac our wounded and killed displayed heroism every time they answered our calls. They were definitely a special breed of warrior. Their ability to land in all kinds of terrain whether under fire or not was phenomenal. The first time that I was med-evaced, doc had stabilized me and given me a shot of morphine prior to being evacuated. I was feeling no pain. I heard a helicopter getting close to our position and realized it was a med-evac chopper hovering above our hastily marked landing zone. As it lowered itself through the haze of the smoke grenade, I noticed two big eyes staring at me. I thought maybe that the shot doc had given me was causing me to see things. It was a bit unnerving until it dawned on me that someone had painted an eyeball on each side of the front of a Sikorsky H-34 helicopter. The H-34 chopper was kind of fat looking compared to the sleek Bell UH-1 (Huey) helicopter. My fire team placed me on my poncho and loaded me up on the chopper. I was flown to the Da Nang Field Hospital. Corpsmen unloaded me off the chopper and onto a stretcher. I looked up at the chopper and saw the pilot looking down at me. I could see the compassion and worry in his eyes. I thanked him by smiling at him and saluting him. He smiled back at me, returned my salute and gave me a thumbs up signal. As the chopper slowly rose into the night sky, the two eyes painted on the front of it gradually disappeared from sight.

The corpsmen placed me on a large concrete floor in the triage tent. Blood was everywhere and the floor was completely covered with wounded men on stretchers. It appeared that our aggressive patrolling to contain V.C. and N.V.A. activities were filling up our field hospitals with wounded. Subdued moaning and groaning could be heard all around me. Occasionally, a corpsman, nurse or doctor would check our vital signs. One of the corpsmen explained to me that the most seriously wounded were worked on first. He gave me another shot of morphine and told me that they would eventually get to everyone. The morphine must have knocked me out cold, because when I woke up, I was not on the concrete floor of the triage tent. I was in a hospital ward full of wounded men. My left leg was in some kind of sling and elevated. I had bandages on my legs, arms and left buttock. Amazingly, I was not in any pain. My left leg and the sling it was resting in, bothered me a bit and I was hoping nothing was broken. On the plus side, I was in a comfortable bed with clean sheets and I could smell the food they were pushing on a cart to each patient. Compared to where I had been and what I had done over the last forty-five days or so, I must be in Heaven. Ha!

My feel-good moment was about to be shattered! I think everyone should know the definition of the word, debridement. Not! Debridement is the cutting of harmful flesh from a wound or the removal of dead, damaged or infected tissue from a wound. Nice word, eh? After I had partaken of the nice, hot, delicious meal brought to me in my nice hospital bed with the nice smelling, clean sheets, I was given a shot for pain. As the corpsman was giving me the pain shot, he asked me what I thought my pain level was, using a scale of one through ten with ten being the worse pain and one being the less pain. I responded that my pain level was about a three or four. He said that was pretty good, but he was giving me a little boost to help me get through my wound debridement. Silly me said thanks, I appreciate it, but what does wound debridement mean? He said everyone with wounds like mine had to have their wounds debrided and not to worry about it. The Marine in the bed next to mine started laughing and told me to get ready, because I would never, ever forget the experience of having my wounds debrided. Now I was worried! I had watched as patients were wheeled into an examination room on a gurney and had heard some muffled screams coming from the examination room. When the patients had been wheeled back into the ward, they were usually out cold and had sweat streaked faces. I told myself to quit worrying. Everyone else was able to get through whatever they were doing to them in that examination room and I could get through it too. Yeah, right!

Finally, my turn came to be loaded on the gurney and wheeled into the examination room. To say that I was nervous would be the understatement of the century. I asked the Lord to give me strength and the fortitude to be able to withstand whatever was about to happen to me. As I was saying a prayer for the corpsmen, nurses and doctors that took care of us, a nurse told me that they had to take the gauze out of my wounds and debride them. She said that I might feel a little pain. I watched as they started pulling the gauze out of a large hole in my leg. If the size of that wound wasn't disconcerting enough, when they got to the gauze that was stuck against the wound, resistance is what they called it, I felt the most excruciating pain that I have ever felt in my life. There is probably worse pain known to man, but I will have to put it right up there or beyond the pain I experienced with a kidney stone later on in my life. I made it through the first wound, but when they started on the rest of them, I broke into a sweat and mercifully passed out. Thank you, Lord! When I woke up, I was back in the hospital ward on my bed. The Marine in the bed next to me that had laughed about what was about to happen to me, was smiling at me and asked me what I thought of them apples. I told him to kiss my a--! That got several of the other wounded guys around us laughing. After a couple of seconds, I started laughing with them. A corpsman was walking by as we were laughing and mumbled something about a bunch of crazy Marines. That just made it worse. It took us awhile to settle down. I guess you could say we had a morbid sense of humor, but I realized the bond we were sharing in that hospital ward started in boot camp. It was ground into our very souls with every step we took on patrol, with every fire fight we fought in, with every wound we suffered together and with all the horrible scenes imbedded in our minds forever. Vietnam had been seared into our very souls. We were brothers. Semper Fi Marine!

After a few days at the Da Nang Field Hospital, several of us were deemed stabilized enough to be transferred to the Hospital Ship U.S.S. Repose via helicopter. X-rays of my left leg had revealed no broken bones and my leg was no longer in traction. A nurse had informed me that they put my leg in traction because of the extensive damage and they did not want me moving it. The hospital ship was basically a smaller version of the hospital ward at the field hospital. Every square inch of space was utilized on the ship. It did not take us long to get used to it. On about the tenth day after I was wounded, they had me up and walking. My left leg was pretty sore and hurt a little when I walked, but not very bad. The minor wounds on my right leg, arms and left buttock did not really bother me. They were healing up nicely. The painful debridement sessions were over and my legs had been sewn up with what looked like fishing line big enough to haul in a whale. The doctor had even told me I would be rejoining my unit in a couple of weeks, barring no unforeseen infection problems. He said that because I had been in good physical shape before I was wounded, coupled with the regimen of good medical attention I was receiving, along with all the good, fresh salt air I was breathing, I should heal up quickly. I have to tell you that although his prognosis was rosy, this was not exactly the vacation cruise of a life time, but it was nice to be ambulatory and be allowed to walk outside along the deck.

I passed the time watching the crazy antics of fish swimming alongside the ship and watched birds sailing along on unseen air currents, occasionally swooping down to grab a fish with their beaks. I would visit with other patients and write or read letters for those that could not use their hands or see. It was a humbling experience. Looking at and talking to some of the other wounded patients made me realize how lucky I had been. Thank you, Lord! One Navy airplane mechanic that had been mangled pretty badly in an accident on an aircraft carrier, was wrapped up in gauze and casts over pretty much all of his body. Several of us wrote letters for him and read to him. All of the medical staff worked hard to help him get stabilized enough to be transferred to a stateside Naval Hospital. When the time came for him to be transferred, he told all of us that he really appreciated us and the time we spent with him. Tragically, we heard that he was killed in a med-evac helicopter crash as they were transferring him. That hit everyone pretty hard.

My mail caught up with me about the second week I was on the U.S.S. Repose. I was sitting up in my bunk reading a Louis L'Amour western when someone shouted out my name and told me I had mail. Much to everyone's surprise, two large, orange colored mail bags were dumped on the deck next to my bunk. There were hundreds of letters in each bag. I could not believe it. When I opened one of the bags and looked at the letters, I realized I did not know most of the people that had written me. Out of all those letters, the very first letter I pulled out of the bag was from my aunt Joanne. Amazing! After I read a few letters, it appeared to me that someone back home had started a letter campaign when they saw the notification of me being wounded in the Shelby County, Alabama newspaper. One of our nurses suggested that I divide up the letters amongst all of the wards, medical staff and ship crew and that is exactly what happened. I think everyone enjoyed reading the letters. I never have figured out who started that letter drive, but I do know it was much appreciated. To all of my family and friends that sent me letters and care packages while I was away from home, I want to say thank you and to tell you that I love you. The letters and care packages were really appreciated not only by me but also by everyone I shared them with. Believe it or not, some guys did not receive anything from home. It was sad, but true. Sharing those letters and care packages really brightened up their day. Many of them could not wait to read my letters and felt they were part of my family. The Lord does work in mysterious ways. Thank you, Lord!

About fifteen days after I was transferred to the U.S.S. Repose, I was discharged back to my unit on light duty. Ha! I still had a few stitches in me, but I knew that did not mean anything. The grasp of the old green weenie was too strong to allow light duty to exist in this man's Marine Corps. Oorah! Marine Corps! A H-34 med-evac helicopter ferried me from the U.S.S. Repose to the Da Nang military airfield with orders to report to the receiving area for transportation to my unit's bivouac area. While I was on my way to receiving, I heard someone calling my name. He was calling me Jimmy, so I figured it was someone from my squad or possibly from back home. When I saw who was calling out my name, I realized it was Alton Srygley, someone I knew from Shelby County, Alabama. His brother Walston, was a classmate of mine in high school. Alton asked me where I was going. I told him that I was checking in at receiving to go back to my unit. He said to forget about that and to come with him. I asked him if I would get in trouble and he said no. Alton was a corporal, so I figured he knew the system a lot better than me. He laughed and said it would be a day or two before the knuckleheads at receiving would be looking for me and if I checked in now, they would probably put me on some kind of crappy work detail. I told him about the first time I checked in at receiving and the poop burning detail I had been put on. Alton laughed and said that he could help me avoid that nonsense.

We went to a nearby Marine engineering unit compound. There was another Shelby County Marine attached to the engineering unit. His name was Terry Kuntsler. Terry had a great set up akin to what Donald Sutherland and his cohorts had in the "MASH" movie. Terry told us to "make ourselves at home." I relaxed and had a hamburger, an order of fries and a milk shake at the Da Nang base PX. It was surreal, like another world and definitely nothing like what I had been doing, or where I had been patrolling before I was wounded. It felt like I was looking through the looking glass in Oz again.

I stayed in the engineering compound a couple of days before Alton advised me to check in at receiving.

When I checked in at receiving, nothing was said about where I had been and I offered nothing to them just like Alton said to do. Sergeants and corporals are pretty smart when it comes to navigating the system. I caught a ride on a "six-by" truck to my battalion area and rejoined my squad. The Tet New Year offensive was in full swing with my battalion aggressively patrolling and engaging Charlie on a daily basis. Less than two weeks after rejoining my squad, I was wounded again. I was blown off of a M-60 tank by a rocket propelled grenade, taken to a nearby landing zone, loaded on a CH-47 (Chinook) med-evac chopper and was med-evaced to Cam Rahn Bay Field Hospital. Fortunately, the holes in me this time were not as big as before. Thank you, Lord! The medical staff extricated the shrapnel that needed to be taken out of me, cleaned my wounds and sewed me up. After X-raying my shoulder, the doctor told me that my corpsman had done a nice job of putting my dislocated shoulder back in place. He said I would need to keep my shoulder in a sling for a couple of days because of the trauma to the shoulder, but otherwise I was in pretty good shape.

That night I was able to sleep in another hospital bed, but I was really wired up. When I woke up the next morning a Catholic priest was sitting in a chair by my bed holding my hand and praying. He said that I was shouting out in my sleep and he felt that I needed someone to pray for me. I told him that I appreciated him praying for me because I was really struggling with my fears. He told me that all the terrible things I had witnessed could be attributed to the flawed nature of man. He said that God was hard at work strengthening every man and woman to overcome their fears and weaknesses. He pointed out that when men let fear reign in their lives, the devil and his minions move in, exacerbating the power of the chaos and carnage that caused me to be fearful. He was so right. He prayed a prayer for the healing of my wounds and the assuaging of my fears. I was at the field hospital for a couple of days before I was discharged back to my unit on light duty. The Crotch's idea of light duty is a lot different than what Jimmy and the doctor's idea of light duty is. Ha! At least I did not have as many stitches in me this time and they were small stitches compared to the whale fishing line they sewed me up with the first time. After I was discharged from the field hospital, a H-34 med-evac helicopter ferried me to my unit's bivouac area. When I got back to my unit, I was told to collect my gear and get myself ready to rejoin my squad. So much for light duty! I went on patrol that night. Doc told me that he would keep an eye on me to make sure none of my wounds got infected. Miraculously, nothing got infected. Ooh Rah! Marine Corps!

Hospital Ship - U.S.S. Repose

10

U.S. Naval Hospital, Agana Guam

The third and last time I was med-evaced turned out to be a long ordeal. I was med-evaced to the Cam Rahn Bay Field Hospital on a Uh-1 (Huey) chopper. At the Cam Rahn Bay Field Hospital, they treated the residual problems associated with all of my wounds. Some of my wounds were healing up nicely but were still in need of additional medical treatment. Physical therapy was started on my left knee. A doctor told me that my knee was not responding positively to the physical therapy. More X-rays of my left knee revealed pieces of shrapnel that needed to be surgically removed. The doctor told me that any other damage to the knee would be corrected when they surgically removed the shrapnel and that they were going to med-evac me to the U.S. Naval Hospital in Agana, Guam for surgery. I was loaded up on a "Starlifter" C-141 med-evac configured jet airplane and was med-evaced to Guam via the Philippines. We had a two night lay over at Clark Air Force Hospital near Manila in the Philippines. Finally, we arrived at Anderson Air Force Base in Guam and were loaded on an ambulance bus for the short trip to the U.S. Naval Hospital in Agana, Guam.

I was admitted to the orthopedics wing of the huge hospital. The orthopedics wing had fifty or more beds, a large bathroom with showers, an examination room, several private rooms, a large recreation room and an ambulatory wing with a lot of bunk beds. All of the beds in the ward, the private rooms and the ambulatory area were full. There were a lot of wounded guys in the orthopedics wing and we were just one wing of many. I was amazed at the number of patients and medical staff within the hospital. After more examinations and x-rays, I was told that I needed some shrapnel removed from the ankle area of my left foot and that would be addressed when my knee was operated on. If that was not bad enough, I was informed that aggressive treatment addressing my malaria and intestinal parasite problems would start some time shortly after my operation. My first question to the doctor that was telling me all this great news was: "What malaria?" My second question was: "What intestinal parasites?" The doctor told me not to worry. He said that most of the wounded they treated were infected with malaria, worms, or parasites. Dad gum Vietnam! The doctor told me that they had medicine that would get rid of my malaria and the parasites. Thank goodness for good Navy medical facilities and good Navy medical staffs.

My operations were deemed successful and I started my recovery phase with my leg in a sling again. They wanted me immobile for a couple of weeks. Can you say I hate bed pans? At least I had no wounds that needed to be debrided. I was really uncomfortable, but it was kind of hard to complain or feel sorry for yourself when a guy on one side of you was terribly wounded with an amputated leg and on the other side of you was a guy that had been shot several times in the legs and torso. Sometimes the Lord works in mysterious ways and there are other times he knocks you over the head with the obvious! The Lord was pointing out to old Jimmy what humility is and was showing me there were many things worse than my own problems. It was an honor to write letters or read to the wounded guys that could not hold a pen or read a book because of their wounds.

Eventually, I was out of traction and able to get in a wheel chair and sit on a pot again. Ah, the pleasures of life! Of course, the old green weenie is always waiting for a good Marine to mess with. It visited me in the form of a humongous pill loaded with what smelled like used motor oil and tasted terrible. The pill was the first dose of the medicine used to convince all of my parasite friends, their babies and their eggs to get the heck out my intestines. The treatment lasted a couple of weeks and I had to catch my poop in a container for someone in the lab to verify that all of the critters were out of my system. How would you like to have that lab job? Ha! The used motor oil smelling stuff worked because I got a clean bill of health in the worm and parasite category of what the heck more can Vietnam do to me. I really should not have asked that question, because about the time I got rid of my parasites, my malaria decided to visit me with a vengeance. Thank goodness the parasite and malaria issues were not a factor while on patrol in Vietnam. That would have been interesting, along with the other nice things like the "trots" and people trying to kill us. Come to think about it, we probably had the trots because of the doggone parasites.   Dad gum Vietnam!

When I was told about my blood work indicating a malaria problem, I wondered why I had not noticed any symptoms.   I could not remember anything specific.   Well, not to worry, I found out quickly how it would affect me right there in that hospital ward.   I could not have been in a better place for the malaria to act up.   I guess it was waiting on my body to be free of parasites where it could get my complete attention or something.   One night I woke up sweating and freezing at the same time.   I asked the nurse for a couple of blankets and when she looked at me, she proceeded to take my temperature and told a couple of corpsmen to get the tub and ice ready for me. I totally misunderstood, because I told her I was freezing, not burning up. She told me that my body temperature was dangerously high, and they needed to get me cooled down immediately.   By that time, I was seeing two of her, was mumbling and did not really care about anything.   When I came around, I was in a tub of ice and turning blue, but at least I wasn't shaking uncontrollably.   Then I realized I was in a tub of ice and started shaking uncontrollably.   I told them I was really cold and asked if I could just go back to bed.   After what seemed like an eternity, they got me out of the tub of ice, dried me off and put me back in bed.   I could not feel anything.   Fortunately, my body responded positively to the drugs they gave me for the malaria.   I had no more sweating and freezing episodes.   The crazy thing about my malaria was I did not exhibit any problems with it until "the night of the ice tub."   Sounds like a good title for a horror story.   Ha!   Dad gum Vietnam!

With the parasite and malaria problems out of the way, I started aggressive physical therapy on my ankle and leg.   To pass the time, we would have wheel chair and gurney races.   Everyone was sworn to secrecy and if anyone hurt themselves the nurse or corpsmen were told that they slipped and fell in the bathroom.   One of our really challenging games was to get to the top of a flight of stairs in your wheelchair without dumping over backwards.   Not many could do it and if you did, there was that little problem of getting back down.   Then there was the knock the other guy on crutches down before he could knock you off your crutches game and everyone's favorite, the sword fights with canes.   Several of us were threatened with a court-martial, but nothing ever happened.   I think the doctors and nurses wrote us off as incorrigible.   Most of the corpsmen wrote us off as a bunch of crazy Marines. They all were probably right on target with their thinking.   Although we were full of mischief and our antics caused them a bit of grief, we thought our doctors, nurses and corpsmen were jewels, deserving of a place in Heaven. The acts of valor performed saving lives on the battlefield and in our military hospitals by our doctors, nurses and corpsmen were many and often. Their courage and fortitude were incredible. They saved a lot of lives and have not been recognized enough for their sacrifices. They witnessed the horrific results of the fighting in Vietnam up close and personal. Their minds are indelibly marked because of what they saw and had to do to save lives. Just as I think that the corpsmen that served with us in the field were the bravest of the brave, I would be remiss if I did not extend that same honor to the brave doctors, nurses and corpsmen that took care of us in the hospitals.

Towards the end of my physical therapy sessions, I got word of the recent death of my dad. One of the Red Cross ladies that served at our hospital brought me a telegram notifying me of his death. I was still on crutches but had made progress walking without crutches with the use of a cane. My doctor asked me if I thought I was up to the trip and I said yes. He asked me to go to the emergency exit and walk up the steps and back down the steps using the crutch. He said it should not be too much trouble for an idiot that tried to go up and down them in a wheel chair. Busted! He smiled at me and told me he knew all about the stupid antics me and some of the other brain-dead idiots were doing. Furthermore, he said if he ever heard of me pulling any other stupid stunts using United States Navy equipment that he would personally come to the ward and kick my rear end all the way to the brig. He was a pretty big man and I had no doubt in my mind that he could back up his words. He asked me if I understood him and what would happen to me if I disobeyed his orders. I stood at attention and told him: "Aye Aye, Sir!" I have to admit it was a pretty good butt chewing for a Navy medical officer and he definitely got my attention. I satisfactorily performed all the tasks he asked me to do and he signed the paper work for me to go home for twenty-one days of emergency leave not charged to my regular leave time. Sweet! I reported to the supply clerk and was issued a couple pairs of new khaki pants, shirts, cap and belt along with new underwear, socks, shoes and accoutrements at no cost to me. The waist size of my pants was an inch smaller than the last pair I had been issued. The supply clerk advised me to get them the same size as my old measurements because I would probably gain weight while I was home on leave. Was he ever right about that! When I returned to the hospital three weeks later my pants were a little tight from all of the good home cooked meals.

I made it home just in time for my dad's funeral. His alcoholism caused a lot of unnecessary grief for him and my family. At the time, I had no respect for him and felt little love for him. That was not fair to him because I was really mad at the alcoholism and how it had affected our family. It took me many years before I resolved that issue and when I did, I knew that I did care for him and love him. I despised what the alcohol did to him. He just did not have the will power to walk away from it. During the funeral and at the graveside service, I tried to cry for him, but I could not. I really felt bad about that and wrote it off as maybe a by-product of combat or something. I spent the night at my sister Mavis' house. She had invited me to stay with her and her family at their house in Montevallo, Alabama. I was pretty restless about everything that had gone on around me and it was kind of a shock to be home. That night I kept getting up and "checking my perimeter" by looking out the windows for movement. My sister heard me stirring around and came up from behind me touching my shoulder. I immediately turned around and grabbed her, trying to choke her. When it dawned on me what I was doing I let her go and we just stared at each other. I told her I was so sorry. I knew she was afraid, but she talked to me and settled me down. I was so ashamed. Lamely, I told her I thought she was a V.C. sneaking up on me and that I had been checking the perimeter outside the window for movement. That did not happen again while I was home, and I was glad of that. I love my sister Mavis.

My emotions got the best of me when I went home with mom. There was a time there in Vietnam when I thought I would never see Simmsville, Alabama again. I was so happy to see everyone and ate like I had not eaten in months. I asked mom if I could borrow dad's car to drive around in while I was home. It was a beautiful 1963 Chevrolet Impala painted a deep, red color with a 327 engine, an automatic transmission with the gear shift in the floor board and bucket seats. Sweet! Mom gave me dad's keys to the car and told me to be careful. Later, mom asked me if I was interested in taking up the payments on the car and I said yes. I figured it was only a matter of time before the Marines sent me stateside to a new duty station and I would need a vehicle to take the place of my old Chevrolet cars that had been sold by my sister Patt while I was away from home. I drove dad's car while I was home and started sending money home to mom to make the monthly payments as soon as I got back to Guam.   Later, when I was ordered to report to Camp Lejeune, North Carolina I was able to drive my car to the base.   That was really nice.

After about a week at home, I felt myself starting to relax and was really enjoying my leave time.   I felt a little pain, but it was not bad enough to use any of the pain pills the doctor had prescribed for me before I started my emergency leave time.   Surprisingly, I did not need to take any of the pain pills while I was home.   I was beginning to realize that I was going to be alright and would be able to handle whatever the Marines had in store for me. It was a very enlivening feeling.   I felt that what I had survived would forever be a part of me and yet I knew that I could now go forward to accomplish more things than I had ever dreamed of doing.   Unfortunately, my twenty-one days of leave was over before I was ready for it to be over and I had to go back to Guam.

As usual, it was hard saying good bye to everyone.   I really love my family. I noticed on the way back to Guam that I was kind of excited and was thinking about my future after I was dismissed from the hospital.   I had thought about a career in the Marines before Vietnam, now I was thinking about college and a life after the Marines.   It appeared to me that the Lord was doing another one of those mysterious works in me.   If the Lord could help me survive combat in Vietnam, then the Lord could help me handle pretty much anything thrown at me in the future.   Thank you, Lord!   I reported back to the hospital and was assigned a lower bunk bed in the ambulatory ward.   I could really see positive results as a result of my physical therapy sessions and it was not too long before I was walking and running again.   I was discharged from the hospital with orders to report to the Marine barracks on Guam.

An Admiral Awarding Me The Purple Heart

U.S. Naval Hospital - Agana, Guam

11

Marine Barracks - Naval Communications Station, Guam

After I was discharged from the hospital, I was placed on light duty and attached to the Marine Barracks on Guam. Since I was on light duty, I was sent to the transportation office to get a military driver's license. For a while after I was issued my license, I drove an officer around. That was pretty good duty and I actually enjoyed the time spent driving and talking to him. When it was found out I had scuba diving experience and was a certified diver, I was sent to work at the special services shop to help with recreation activities offered at the base. That was excellent duty! I got to eat at the sub base chow hall. It was probably the best chow hall on Guam. Between my physical training and my weekly physical therapy sessions, I was experiencing some pretty good pain. I took the pills that the doctor had prescribed, but they were not helping a lot, so I started to augment the pain pills with a few shots of Jim Beam whiskey pretty regularly. That was a bad mistake on my part because it took me down a thirty to forty-five-day flirt with drug and alcohol abuse.

During this time, I got to re-qualify with the M-14 rifle. I shot high expert and nearly broke the existing range record. My light duty status was lifted, and I was rated fit for full duty. With full duty status came a transfer to guard duty at the Naval Communications Center on Guam. I started regular physical training with my platoon. After a few runs and calisthenics sessions, I realized I was not in good physical shape. I really struggled on the runs and some of the calisthenics were hard to do. When I had been at the Naval communications center about a month, I could tell was getting back in pretty good shape. I was able to run and perform calisthenics a lot easier. I also noticed that my pain was diminishing, and I was starting to feel normal again.

While shaving one morning, I noticed the pain pills and the pint of Jim Beam whiskey in my ditty bag and realized I had a problem that I needed to address immediately. I crushed all of the pain pills and flushed them down the commode. I gathered up another pint of whiskey that I had in my foot locker and poured it and the pint in my ditty bag in the sink and washed them down the drain. Whatever bacteria or animal living in the sewer system would soon be feeling no pain. I did not completely stop drinking, but I drastically cut back and have never drank like that again. The next time I had a doctor's appointment, I told him what I had done and asked him to cancel my pain pill prescription. He told me that he was proud of me talking to him about my flirt with alcohol and drug abuse, recommending that I follow my conscious concerning drinking and that he would cancel the prescription. I felt energized and was getting my happy spirit back. Thank you, Lord! Looking back, I realized that a lot of things had happened to me in a short period of time and that the influence of my faith and my family had kicked in when I needed it to kick in. The devil had been at work within old Jimmy and knew I was weak. He saw I was ripe for abuse. I replaced the prescription pain medicine and drinking with exercising, running and getting back to taking care of my mind, body and soul.

My guard duty at the Naval Communications Station, Guam, lasted about two months before I was ordered to report for duty at Camp Lejeune, North Carolina. At Camp Lejeune, I was transferred out of the infantry and assigned to brig guard training at the Base Brig. Before I left Guam, I was promoted to corporal. With my promotion to corporal, I received a nice pay raise with more privileges like registering and driving my own personal transportation on base. Yes!

Rifle Range - Guam

12

Camp Lejeune

I was allowed ten days leave while in route to Camp Lejeune that was not charged to my leave time. I went straight to Simmsville, Alabama and stayed with mom at the farm for a few days. It was really nice to see everyone again. I spent two or three days on the beach at Panama City, Florida and went scuba diving a couple of times. By the time my leave was over, I was looking forward to what the future had in store for me and could not wait to get to Camp Lejeune. I paid off the loan on my car, bought car insurance, renewed my Alabama driver's license, purchased my car tags and made sure I had everything I needed to register my car at Camp Lejeune.

When I arrived at Camp Lejeune, I registered my car and placed the base decals on the windshield of my car. I turned in my orders and was assigned living quarters at a barracks near the brig. My platoon sergeant and company gunny talked with me and explained the training schedule I would be going through. The training schedule was basically on the job training and turned out to be pretty interesting. After about two weeks of training, I was told that I would be the quarter deck NCO in charge of checking prisoners in and assigning them to their quarters. The base brig had large, open cells that housed different categories of prisoners ranging from minimum custody through medium custody to maximum custody depending on their infractions. We also had several isolation cells for those prisoners that had committed serious crimes or needed to be isolated from the general prison population. Everything was strictly regulated with special attention paid to the safety of the prisoners and brig staff. At first, I was amazed at some of the infractions that were committed by different prisoners, but I also knew that Marine customs and courtesies were inviolate. They would be observed, or you would pay a price, like thirty days in the brig for failure to salute or show the proper respect. A stateside, non-war zone Marine was expected to act and look like a Marine, no exceptions! For some that came back from Vietnam it was a rude awakening, as the R.E.M.F.s ruled at stateside billets.

There were a few non-commissioned officers (NCOs) and officers at Camp Lejeune that had not seen combat and did not have very many ribbons denoting their service on their manly chests. They made a lot of unnecessary remarks or abused their positions by provoking Marines with several ribbons denoting their combat service to do or say something that would get them in trouble. We called it playing "Mickey Mouse" games with us. It was a shame, but it happened. Most Marines served their brig time, rejoined their units and had no further problems. A few of the Marines that were incarcerated, really spiraled out of control into a life of petty crime and contempt towards other Marines. These were the ones we had to watch closely. Some of them were in for thirty days and would cause so much grief that they would earn more time in the brig. It was really frustrating to watch them degenerate into a criminal mind set. Perhaps some were already that way before they joined the Marines, or they just did not care. Some were looking for administrative or dishonorable discharges. They could make weapons from razor blades, spoons, forks or any other thing they could get their hands on. You had to really pay close attention to them when you were breaking up fights or inspecting cells. It was crazy what some prisoners would do. They made life hard on everyone around them over some of the most petty things imaginable. The incredible thing was how some were incarcerated for thirty days or less and could literally develop a criminal mindset. Sad!

One of the Marines I checked in at the brig was a member of my boot camp platoon at Parris Island. He was from Sulligent, Alabama. I had seen him at the Birmingham, Alabama airport when I was headed back to Guam, after my emergency leave. He really looked sharp in his uniform with a Force Recon Badge, Paratroopers Wings and a salad bowl of ribbons including the Silver Star and Bronze Star. His countenance was a credit to the Marine Corps. We talked for about an hour while waiting on our planes to load passengers. I asked him about his Purple Heart ribbon with oak leaf clusters indicating that he had been wounded several times. He told me that he had healed up pretty good with no complications. I was really impressed with him and his accomplishments. Based on what he told me, he was lucky to be alive.

I had been at Camp Lejeune about two months and was up to my elbows in paperwork when a Marine approached my desk and laid his orders and military record file on my desk. When I looked up it was the Marine from Sulligent, Alabama. I asked him what he was up to and if he was going to be assigned to our brig staff. He looked kind of confused and then I noticed the brig guard escorting him and realized he was going to be a prisoner at the brig. I asked him what he had done to get brig time. He said he had deserted. I could not believe it and asked him why he would do that. He said that he did not want to go to Vietnam. I told him I could understand that after what he had seen and been through the first time in Vietnam. He told me that he had never been in Vietnam and that he had deserted while on leave after advanced infantry training. Wow! I was not expecting that answer. I told him that I was really sorry for the way things had turned out for him. I do not know what happened with him, but if anyone ever deserved brig time, he had definitely earned it. Holy Smokes!

One of the good things about a billet like Camp Lejeune was that I could get passes to leave the base at night or on weekends. Going to Jacksonville, North Carolina at night got to be a regular thing for me and one of my buddies. His name was Lawrence P. Nodine. We called him "Nody." He was from the northeast, I think Connecticut. We had a lot of fun playing pool, drinking beer and eating hot dogs. I think he had memorized every beer label known to man. We won a lot of free beers and hot dogs off of people that would bet he could not recite every word on a beer label. We would wait for our victims to sit at the bar near us and our scam would usually start when I would bet Nody a beer or a hot dog that he could not recite the words on the label of a certain beer bottle. Everyone sitting near us would listen and it never failed to trick someone. We rarely paid for beers or hot dogs. Nody was one funny guy. He had been wounded in Vietnam and was eventually medically discharged because of his wounds. It seemed like most of the Marines that I was stationed with at Camp Lejeune and later on in Hawaii, had been wounded one or more times. Vietnam had been rough on a lot of Marines. The price we paid in Vietnam was pretty apparent to all of us by the scars on our bodies. Another thing I did while I was at Camp Lejeune was to "swoop" home for a couple of days. Basically, I would pick up four or five riders at Camp Lejeune, or Fort Bragg on a Friday, take them to Atlanta, Birmingham or points in-between and back to Camp Lejeune or Fort Bragg on a Sunday for a price. I did this twice a month when I did not have any duty assignments at the brig. It was a pretty sweet deal for me and saved the riders money. The money I received from the riders paid for my expenses, insurance, up-keep on my car and the speeding tickets I had to pay. Every small North Carolina town that had a policeman loved to stop servicemen and write them tickets for any infraction they could think up, cash expected at the time of the stop, of course. That is not to say I did not earn my fair share of them. They had us over a barrel because they knew we did not need them to report our traffic tickets to our commanding officers for fear of losing our driving privileges. All in all, it was a fair trade off because I got to visit my family and girlfriend, plus pay for all of my expenses. Sadly, as they say, all good things must come to an end.

My time at Camp Lejeune came to an end because of a prison riot. Just before we moved into our new brig at Camp Lejeune, we had a pretty bad prison riot. We had experienced fights and racial strife between African American, Latino American and White Supremacist prisoners on and off for a while. We usually settled everyone down and tried to segregate them from each other. One of the riots got out of control and involved hostages in the brig kitchen area. A couple of brig personnel were injured, and we had to go in with nightsticks and shotguns to quell the riot and rescue the hostages. After we regained control of all prison areas, we had to send a few guards and prisoners to the base hospital. The riot got the attention of several congressmen and senators causing an uproar about brig guard brutality that was completely untrue. It was said that the riot had been orchestrated to start simultaneously by prisoners at the Camp Pendleton Marine Brig and the Camp Lejeune Marine Brig because of supposedly terrible conditions at the brigs. The Camp Lejeune brig was old, but I witnessed no terrible conditions nor prisoner mistreatment while I was stationed there.

Not too long after the riot, we moved into our new, modern base brig. It was reputed that no one could escape from the new brig. While prisoners detailed to the prison mess hall were setting up equipment in the kitchen, one of them took the wire cutters they were using to cut shipping restraints off the equipment packaging material and cut a hole in the fence surrounding the brig. Several prisoners escaped. They were quickly caught, but the inescapable new brig idea was put to rest quickly. Not long after that, I was told to report

Page 89

to the company gunny. When I reported to him, he told me several prison guards were going to be transferred due to the prison riot and I was one of them. I asked him if I was in any trouble and he said no. He said I could go to Hawaii, Japan or the Philippines. I told him that I would love to go to Hawaii, and he told me to put Hawaii last and the one I did not want to go to first. I must have looked confused because he told me to trust him and that I ought to know by now the "Crotch" would probably send me anywhere other than where I wanted to go. I looked him in the eye and told him I wanted to go to the Philippines first, Japan second and definitely did not want to go to Hawaii. Two days later I had my orders in hand sending me to LuaLuaLei Naval Ammunition and Communications Depot located on Oahu, Hawaii. I was given ten days travel leave not charged to my leave time. Oorah! Marine Corps!

I packed up all of my gear, loaded it up in my car, said my good byes and headed home for a few days of leave time before I had to catch my flight to Hawaii. Part of me could not wait to see everyone and spend time with them. Another part of me was antsy and ready to experience my new duty station. I needed to get to Hawaii, serve my time and get on with my life. I found myself thinking more and more about what I wanted to do when my enlistment time was over. Scuttlebutt had everyone thinking that you could get discharged early to enter college or some kind of technical training. I had not really thought about that, but I was determined to check out the scuttlebutt as soon as I got settled at my new duty station. While I was home on leave, I put my car up for sale. I knew that I would not need it for over a year or more. Several people were interested, and I was able to sell it quickly at a pretty good price. I gave Mom part of the money and put the rest in my credit union. My sisters, my brother and I have always tried to help our momma in every way we could. All of us knew we could never repay her for all she had done for us. She was a real jewel. Mom took me to the Birmingham, Alabama airport and we said our goodbyes. I told her that I would write her as soon as I got settled.

13

Hawaii

When I arrived at the Honolulu airport, I loaded up on a Navy shuttle bus and it took me to LuaLuaLei. I turned in my orders and was assigned quarters. The next day, after talking with my company commander, I was appointed to one of the Corporal of the guard positions. It was really a great duty station. We basically stood guard, did our required exercises and running, kept our living and working areas cleaned, kept our uniforms and appearances in tip top shape, completed our training schedules and enjoyed some of the best, off duty time known to mankind. We had no trouble getting passes to go off base on our free time. Our company commander (C.O.) told us that if we kept ourselves squared away, stayed out of trouble and performed our duties well, we could get passes to go anywhere on Oahu, or any of the other Hawaiian Islands we wanted to go too. He told us that if any of us got in any trouble, he would do his best to help us out. He was a really good C.O. and we tried to be the best looking, most squared away Marines on Oahu.

Our small base was located in an extinct volcano crater in the Puu Hapapa mountain range. It had housing for officers and senior enlisted, a post office, a dry-cleaners, post exchange, barracks, offices, sick bay, pistol range, recreational facilities and more. The communications station had several buildings, giant antennas and dish antennas, while most of the rest of the base was devoted to ammunition bunkers with their associated buildings, roads and small gauge railway equipment. The railroad was connected to various bases on Oahu. I never saw the railway used. Mostly they moved ammunition and equipment on covered trucks, or trucks with trailers. Scuttlebutt had it that nuclear weapons were stored in some of the bunkers. I figured that was why everyone had to be vetted for secret clearances. If nuclear weapons were stored there, I never saw any while I was there. I guess it is okay for me to mention the scuttlebutt about nuclear weapons storage because contractors were in the process of dismantling the base in March of 2016 when my family and I vacationed on Oahu. The barracks that I lived in was about the only thing left that I recognized.

When I first arrived on base, I was told about a great place to eat that was located near the entrance of our base access road. The small cafe had the best beans and rice I have ever tasted. As corporal of the guard and later as sergeant of the guard, I ate many meals there. The cafe was located at a turn-around area our patrol vehicles used. Near the check-out counter of the cafe, they sold maps of the local area. There was a map that showed our base and it pretty accurately showed all of the base facilities and ammunition bunkers. So much for secret clearances! "X" marked the spot. Ha! Aloha, Hawaii!

Another interesting thing about our base was the large cross at the top of Kole Kole Pass. It supposedly marked where the ancient Hawaiians threw virgins into the volcano to appease Pele, the goddess of fire, lightning, wind and volcanoes. Supposedly, the Japanese also used the pass to vector in on Pearl Harbor when they attacked Pearl Harbor on December 7, 1941. I do not know if this was true or not. There were several entrances to our base, but we only used two regularly. The front gate used an entrance road off of the main highway out of Honolulu towards Waianae in the southwest part of Oahu and the back gate was located at the top of Kole Kole Pass. The road from our back gate at Kole Kole Pass led to an army base called Schofield Barracks. Another gate near the Naval Communications Station was used occasionally. We did not have a permanent guard stationed at that gate. We had observation towers and checkpoints that were manned twenty-four hours a day, seven days a week. Guards were armed with pistols and M-14 rifles. Some towers were designed for the use of M-60 machine guns. Anyone entering or leaving the base was subject to inspection. We rigorously enforced traffic rules and wrote a lot of traffic tickets. The manned observation towers monitored traffic on the road from the front gate to the rear gate twenty-four hours a day. No unauthorized admittance to restricted areas was permitted. I never asked what kind of ammunition was stored in the ammunition bunkers and figured it was none of my business.

Not long after I arrived on base, I entered my name in a raffle at the enlisted men's Club and won the right to register in my name, a beautiful, 1955

Chevrolet convertible while I was stationed on Oahu. This car had been passed on year to year to a different Sailor or Marine depending on who won the raffle. I had to register the car in my name at the Hawaiian Motor Vehicle Department in Honolulu, Hawaii and buy car insurance to cover any accidents. I was responsible for the upkeep of the car, including any repair work needed, oil changes, tires, batteries and gas. That was not a problem because anyone that used the car with my permission paid me for the use of it. I was given more than enough money to cover all expenses encountered while I had possession of the car. It was a sweet deal. That was one pampered car. I passed it on to another Marine that won the yearly raffle just before I left Hawaii. I have often wondered whatever happened to that car.

When we were not on duty, performing personal hygiene chores, training, exercising or running, we were usually at one of the nearby beaches, the LuaLuaLei enlisted men's club, Waianae Army Recreation Center, Pearl Harbor enlisted men's club, Honolulu, Waikiki, or visiting interesting areas around Oahu. Generally, our free time at any of these areas revolved around women, beer and the pursuit of happiness. Ha! The first time some of my so-called buddies took me to Waikiki for a night on the town, they really pulled a good one on me. At one of the clubs we went to, I noticed that a couple of nice-looking girls were acting very friendly and were smiling at me. I naturally started talking to them and even danced with one of them. I noticed my buddies were nearly laughing uncontrollably at something and thought someone had told a good joke. After the music stopped, I decided to go to the bathroom. Well surprise, surprise if old Jimmy had not walked into the ladies bath room…but wait a minute, there were urinals and the girl using the urinal wasn't a girl! Needless to say, I quickly realized my buddies had played a trick on me and I was the joke they were laughing at. We were at a drag queen bar. The locals called them mahu or mahunies. Talk about embarrassing! My so-called buddies got a good laugh at my expense. I vowed to get even with them and over the next thirteen months I managed to pull a pretty good prank on all of them. I knew that I was supposed to turn the other cheek, but pay back is really sweet, sometimes. Ha! After that little episode old Jimmy tried to patronize the various enlisted men's clubs and avoid civilian clubs.

Usually, the enlisted men's clubs were scenes of brawls between the Navy, Army and the Marines. No one tried to seriously hurt anyone and most of the time everyone involved in the brawl would end up buying each other drinks. Sometimes the brawls got out of hand and we had to quickly depart the club before the Shore Patrol or Military Police arrived at the scene. We did not have to worry about brawls, shore Patrol or Military police at our LuaLuaLei enlisted men's club because fighting was forbidden. The Hawaiian lady that managed our club strictly enforced the no fighting rule with no exceptions. She was a really nice lady but a tough little cookie that would let you know quickly who was in charge of our club. She would entertain us with a luau every now and then. We were always bringing her wild pigs that we caught on base. There was definitely no shortage of wild pigs running around the base. Occasionally, piglets would become orphans because their mother came out on the short end of a traffic accident or they would get separated from their mother. Whenever we saw a piglet or piglets without their mother around, we would catch all of them we could. It was in your best interest to make sure that the piglet's mother was not nearby. An angry wild pig trying to protect a baby piglet was very dangerous and would do whatever necessary to protect her babies. They could hurt you if they could get to you. Several of our patrol vehicles were damaged by irate pigs butting the sides of the vehicles. There were a couple of local Hawaiians that were authorized to let their livestock graze at different areas on the base. One of them would usually dispose of any pigs killed or injured on the base. If they got to the killed or injured pigs in time, they could butcher them and cook them at a luau. Welcome to Hawaii!

We had a couple of Navy guys from the Carolinas that would get with some local Hawaiian guys and hunt wild pigs on our base with hound dogs and knives. After several weeks of badgering me, they convinced me that I needed to join them on a pig hunting expedition. Looking at some of the scars on their arms and legs from up close and personal encounters with wild hogs did not exactly generate a lot of enthusiasm on my part for a pig hunting expedition. After much thought, I decided what the heck, a pig hunting old Jimmy would go! I have to admit that it was pretty exciting to hear and watch the big hound dogs chase and corner a big pig. Some of the boars were huge. They could cut a dog with their tusks and sling it several feet through the air if the tusk hooked the dog just right. If the dog was not injured too badly, one of the hunters would sew up the wound on the spot and the dog would reenter the fray. When the dogs cornered the pig, they would hold onto the pig's ears or neck and wrestle the pig down on the ground. One of the hunters would walk up to the pig and finish it off with a long knife. When my turn came to finish a pig off with the knife, I got close to the pig and it started moving towards me, dragging the dogs. I had brought my pistol with me in case of an emergency. That pig with those gigantic tusks coming at me was as close to an emergency as I have ever seen. I dropped the knife, pulled out my pistol and shot the pig. The other hunters were pretty disgusted with me. I pointed out that one of them had a shotgun for emergencies. I definitely did not want to be between a charging wild pig and a shotgun if they decided it was an emergency. They were mad at me for endangering their dogs. Even the dogs looked at me pretty disgustingly. One of the hunters said I had ruined the head and brains. Really? Needless to say, I was never invited back on a wild pig hunt again. I cannot say as I missed it much, either!

I really enjoyed scuba diving and snorkeling in Oahu, Maui and Kauai. The water was clear and there were some beautiful reefs with their associated marine wildlife to look at. Makaha beach was not too far from our back gate. We would go there a lot to watch the surfers ride gigantic waves. Several of the Marines that were stationed with me at LuaLuaLei were able to master the surf board, but I was not one of them. On the northeast side of Oahu, we watched wind surfers negotiate dangerous rocks, occasionally wiping out on them. Sometimes they would scrape or gouge themselves pretty badly. That is probably why I never tried wind surfing! On the northwestern end of the Island we would watch gliders float through the air, using the air currents through and around the mountains. It was amazing how they flew the air currents. You would not think they could stay in the air as long as they did without an engine to propel them. Occasionally, we cut pineapples out of a field of pineapples that we felt endangered passing traffic. We just naturally thought the first row by the road was reserved for us. Ha! One fellow caught us and told us not to make a habit of it. That was nice of him. He could have had us arrested. There was a pretty hefty fine for pilfering pineapples. Mixed in between all of our excursions was our continuous admiration shown to the girls we encountered. Hawaii is a beautiful State and was a really hard duty station. Ha! Someone had to fill the available positions and I am glad I got my chance. I have often told people that I went from the hell of Vietnam to the heaven of Hawaii. Oorah! Marine Corps!

All was not a bed of roses at LuaLuaLei. We had occasional fights, a little bit of racial problems and our share of crazoids. Most of the fights were over misunderstandings and were cleared up pretty quickly with any resulting injuries marked off as a bad fall. One time a couple of our resident black power guys tangled with a quiet, unassuming Marine that basically corrected their attitudes by knocking one of them out of a window and the other two around the recreation room until they felt they had all they wanted of the quiet, unassuming Marine. Mostly, we did not have race issues, but a couple of guys felt like they had to press the issue on occasions. Everyone usually ignored them. I saw no one in our platoon start any racial trouble except for our resident black power guys and even then, there was not a lot of racial strife. We did have a couple of white guys that ran their mouths on occasions, but for the most part, everyone ignored all of them.

We had a few guys that really struggled with their wounds and P.T.S.D. Most of the time they handled their problems okay and other times some of us would talk to them. A few went absent without leave (AWOL) and were confined to the brig. What they really needed was counseling. We had one guy freak out in the shower one night and start cutting himself with a razor blade. We got him under control and took him to our on-base sick bay. They stabilized him and sent him to the military hospital in Honolulu. Scuttlebutt had it that he was shipped stateside. Another Marine dropped an ashtray made from the bottom of an artillery shell full of sand on the head of a Jewish corporal that no one much cared for. There was just something about him that made you not want to trust him. I have had many Jewish buddies, so I do not think it was a religious thing. The corporal went to the hospital and did not return and the crazoid Marine that dropped the shell went to the brig. That same crazoid Marine lived in Alabama and later visited my wife Kathy and me when we lived in Montgomery, Alabama. He was still a little wild acting. He wanted us to go bar hopping with him and his girlfriend. I politely declined his offer under the pretext of ongoing obligations. He said okay and left. I never saw him again. I hope he was able to get his life in order.

I had my moments while on Oahu. One night after a night of partying at Pearl Harbor enlisted men's club, I was stopped by the police for driving while intoxicated. During the traffic stop, a fight broke out. There were probably seven or eight of us squeezed in the car and the police called for backup. I will probably never know how many policemen were involved, but they finally subdued us and hauled us to jail. Looking back on the incident, it was not one of my most stellar moments.   Amazingly, the next morning we were let go to the custody of our C.O. and company gunny.   We had to pay fines and the medical bills of the policemen injured.   All of us had knots on our heads and were bruised up a bit.   None of us said a word except for "yes sir" and "no sir" for the thirty or forty minutes we were chewed out by our C.O. and the gunny.   We were lucky.   We got off light.   None of us were allowed any passes off base for thirty days.

Another time I hit a staff sergeant that worked in the company office.   He was a real pain in the rear with the gear office poke.   There were two people at LuaLuaLei that most of us did not trust.   The office poke staff sergeant was one and the Jewish corporal that was hurt with the artillery shell ashtray was the other.   Both of them were overweight and sloppy looking Marines.   That is a rare thing to see in the Marines and everyone thought these guys were possibly Naval Criminal Investigation Service (N.C.I.S.) spies.   Ha!   The staff sergeant and I just did not get along with each other and the gunny warned me to stay away from him because he was trouble.   He had a "Fire Watch" ribbon and a "Good Conduct" ribbon on his manly chest.   Needless to say, he was scorned by most of the company, including me.   We had words a couple of times and I felt he was baiting me, so I tried to avoid him.   One day I was late for formation and he confronted me about it.   I told him that I had informed the gunny that I would be late for formation, but he kept pushing the issue with me and jabbed his finger into my chest.   Like an idiot, I popped him in the jaw with my fist.   I knew I was in trouble as soon as I hit him because he just smiled and walked away.   That afternoon I was standing tall before the colonel getting a real chewing out for conduct unbecoming of a non-commissioned officer.   I lost my sergeant's stripes I was about to pin on and was confined to base for thirty days.   I was lucky I did not get busted down several ranks or get thrown in the brig.   At that point and time, it did not really matter because I was going to be discharged from active duty within thirty days.   I wish I had not fallen for the staff sergeant's trap, but I did.   His intention was to get me to take a swipe at him.   He knew if he goaded me enough and made me do something stupid, I would lose my sergeant's stripes. I really wanted that stripe.   After all was said and done, I knew it was my fault.

It did not take me long to put it behind me because I was already thinking about civilian life and college.   I had applied for an early out program offered for education opportunities. Scuttlebutt was floating around that Marines with purple hearts could get a six month or more early out. It had something to do with a reduction of forces in Vietnam and elsewhere. I was offered nearly thirteen months off my enlistment. I took it! My last thirty days at LuaLuaLei were a blur. I got the paperwork on my car transferred to the new Marine that won the car lottery at the enlisted men's club, turned in my equipment and started packing my clothes. It still amazes me how much you can pack in a sea bag. Before I knew it, I had my airline tickets and orders in my hand instructing me to report to the Treasure Island Navy Yard in San Francisco, California. I was to be discharged from active duty in the Marines. Yes! I was ready to say "Aloha" to Hawaii, but I was hoping I would get a chance to go back to Hawaii one day. It is a really nice experience to be able to close my eyes and see beautiful Hawaii in my mind. Little did I know at the time that I would take my family to Hawaii twice for vacations. I intend to take them back again, if I can. Aloha, Hawaii!

14

Treasure Island and Discharge From The Marines

My orders were to report to the Treasure Island Navy Yard to be discharged from the Marines. Treasure Island is located in the San Francisco Bay between San Francisco and Oakland. I figured that I would turn my orders in, go through my out processing and be headed home in about two or three days. Wrong! You do remember what I have mentioned about getting the old green weenie? Now why would a seasoned Marine like I thought I was, think that the United States Marine Corps would simply discharge a Marine without squeezing a few more days or weeks of labor out of him. Silly me! I spent nearly three stinking weeks on that base out in the middle of the bay. They assigned me to guard duty, mess hall duty, barracks duty and anything else they could milk out of me.

The loss of my sea bag with my complete set of United States Marine Corps clothing issue came back to haunt me at Treasure Island. It was made clear to me that because the Marines had lost my complete issue of clothing on Okinawa, that the Marines were going to make sure they corrected that injustice to me. Remember, the wisdom of the United States Marine Corps is inviolate! I had to go to Camp Pendleton to obtain a complete issue of clothing. Everything went smooth until they got to my boots. I was informed that they did not have my size. I told them I could wear a half size larger. They did not have that size either. I told the issue clerk to just give me any pair of boots because I did not intend to wear them anyway. He informed me that he could not do that. I was told that he would place an order for my boots and have them shipped to me at the Treasure Island Navy Yard. He said that he had no idea how long that would take. Dad gum R.E.M.F.! Oorah! Marine Corps!

Thus, started my several weeks availability for any duties the Marines could think up for me to do. Thank goodness I was able to get off-base passes. That helped salve the indignation to my ego. I could not afford to do a lot, but I had a lot of fun walking and riding around San Francisco. I went to the Fishermen's Wharf, the Cannery, took a ride on a trolley, drove across the Golden Gate Bridge, ate at various restaurants and took in as much of the sights as possible. The attitude of the San Francisco residents I encountered was very laid back. They were a bit on the weird side, but likable. Some of the lifestyles that were accepted ranged from eccentric to perverse. There were a lot of knuckleheaded Vietnam war protesters that tried your patience if they thought you were in the military, but I was pretty successful at ignoring them. Maybe my run-in with that overweight piece of poo-poo staff sergeant at LuaLuaLei had taught me something about controlling myself. Oops! Maybe it did not, but at least I was attempting to change some of my bad habits. As they say, old habits die hard!

My boots that the Marine clothing clerk at Camp Pendleton ordered for me finally arrived and I was able to place a check mark in the block next to the complete set of Marine clothing issue. Hallelujah! It took them over two weeks to get those dad gum boots shipped to me. They were a half size too large, but I was not going to say one thing about that. Old Jimmy was going to be the best turned out Marine on base, observing the customs and courtesies of the United States Marine Corps to the letter. Oorah! Marine Corps! Fortunately for me, everything else concerning my out-processing went as smooth as silk. During my mustering out physical, I was informed that I would be medically discharged and was to report to the Veterans Administration (V.A.) Hospital located in Birmingham, Alabama. One of the Corpsmen told me I would probably get a disability rating because of my wounds and that is why I was being medically discharged to the V.A. Hospital nearest my home. Other than signing some paper work, picking up my airline tickets and drawing my mustering out pay, I was ready to go home. I have to admit I was one happy Jimmy! My mustering out pay included my pay owed me through my discharge date of May 25, 1970, excess leave-pay and incidentals. The total was a lot more than I had expected. Sweet! I had not realized it, but just about all of the leave I had taken while in the Marines had been emergency or travel leave, not charged against my accrued leave time. You might call it poetic justice for all of my "Green Weenie" ordeals while in the Marines. Ha!

After all of my mustering out (discharge) requirements were fulfilled, I went back to the barracks and packed my sea bags. I showed my discharge papers to the sergeant in charge of my barracks, checked out of the barracks and walked through the front gate towards the nearby dedicated taxi stand for the base. I had to walk about two hundred feet from the front gate to the taxi stand. The walk to the taxi stand was a real interesting walk. It was interesting because on both sides of the access road to the base were booths with people representing every law enforcement agency and right-wing or left-wing group known to man. All of them were wanting me to join their agency or group. The irony of it all was amazing. Some of the people on one side of the road had probably arrested some of the people on the other side of the road. Welcome to California! I was glad to be leaving.

A couple of us rented a cab to take us to the airport. As we were crossing the San Francisco - Oakland Bridge over the San Francisco Bay, I feigned an upset stomach and told the cab driver to pull over quick or I was going to get sick in his cab. When he pulled over, I told him to open the trunk where I could get to my medicine. When he opened the trunk, I grabbed one of my sea bags full of new United States Marine Corps clothing issue and threw it over the bridge into the bay. The cab driver could not believe that I threw a sea bag full of clothing into the bay. He was really mad at me when I got back into the cab and told me that I had better hope I did not get arrested for throwing my sea bag into the bay. I told him I was sorry and that I would give him a generous tip. When I got back in the cab, the cab driver did not say another word to any of us. The other Marines in the cab just shook their heads and told me that I was an idiot, pointing out I could have sold all of the uniforms for a couple of hundred bucks. Oops! In hindsight, I wish I had not thrown my sea bag into the bay because my nephews would have loved to get their hands on all of those uniforms. It appeared that I needed to work on controlling my temper a bit more. Thank you for showing me the need for humility, Lord!

When we got to the airport, we paid off the taxi cab driver and I did give him a generous tip as promised. He just mumbled something about crazy Marines. Ha! As we walked towards the ticket counter, we passed a bunch of hippy war protesters that were giving every serviceman that passed by them a piece of their minds. They were cussing at us and spitting on us. A Marine gunnery sergeant that was walking with us said "steady," march right by them and do not pay any attention to them. All of us marched right by them, looking straight ahead and listening to the gunny's marching cadence. No one else bothered us. Some people went out of their way to apologize for the way the hippy crazoids treated us, even going out of their way to yell "shame on you" at the protesters. We went into a nearby restroom and washed the spit off our uniforms and got ourselves squared away. By the time I boarded my plane, my uniform was dry, and I was feeling pretty good about meeting my family at the Birmingham, Alabama airport.

15

Reentering Civilian life

Flying military standby does not guarantee you a seat, but on my flight to the Dallas-Fort Worth airport, I hit the jackpot and was seated in the first-class section next to an elderly African American gentleman. The pilot and co-pilot were Marine aviators. They spotted me as I entered the airplane and went out of their way to ensure that I had the best flight home, ever. They succeeded! To my amazement, not only was I seated in the first-class section, drinks and snacks were continuously placed before me. I asked the elderly gentleman seated next to me if he would like to share some of the items the stewardesses were bringing me as I could not possibly drink nor eat all of it. I managed to stop the flow of snacks, but they never stopped bringing drinks. They even brought a bottle of champagne when they found out I was celebrating my discharge from active duty in the Marines and going home. Needless to say, when we landed at the Dallas-Fort Worth airport in Texas, I was feeling no pain and in a state of euphoria. The elderly gentleman sitting next to me was basically in the same shape. I helped him gather his carry-on luggage, grabbed my carry-on luggage and escorted him to the terminal. Was I surprised when we walked out into our gate terminal area and saw a sea of African American faces standing beneath a giant banner saying: "Welcome home, Grandpa." I ushered him into the loving arms of his family, said goodbye and headed for the terminal that was taking me to Birmingham, Alabama. As I was leaving, he told me that he really enjoyed talking to me and drinking with me. There were a few in the crowd that were not too happy about our euphoric condition. Jimmy was glad he was making a quick exit!

The flight to Birmingham was pretty uneventful and I drank a lot of coffee. I called mom as soon as I could find a phone and told her that I was at the Birmingham airport. She said that she and my sister Patt would pick me up. That was great for me because I needed to clean up a bit in the bathroom and drink about another gallon of coffee to get me back to a somewhat normal condition, minus the extreme euphoria. When my sister Patt found me drinking coffee at the bar, she asked me if I was ready to go home. She gave me "The Look" as soon as she saw me. I think all women learn how and when to use the look as little girls. My sister Patt, being the mature woman that she is, had mastered the art of giving the look to perfection. Ha! We talked the time away as we drove home in the car and when we turned onto Shelby County, Alabama Highway 11, a couple of miles from home, I got pretty emotional. I realized that I was finally safe at home with my family, out of the Marines and no one would be shooting at me again, ever. Hopefully, I could put the memory of Vietnam somewhere else in my mind and get on with my life. I had a lot of unpleasant memories in my mind and a bunch of scars all over my body, but at least I did not have to worry about patrolling, or fighting V.C. or N.V.A. any more.

Unfortunately, the pain from my wounds came back to haunt me in several ways. First, there was the physical pain in my leg that would not go away. Along with the pain in my leg, my shoulder would ache, and I was having some issues with a skin rash that looked like the jungle rot that plagued me in Vietnam. I went to the V.A. hospital in Birmingham and submitted the medical records given to me at Treasure Island Naval Yard. I was examined, given a disability rating and a V.A. identification card. The V.A. doctor that examined me ordered a leg/ankle brace support to help mitigate the pain in my leg. The brace actually helped. I used the brace for a couple of years and managed to get by with no surgery for about two years. The doctor recommended steroid shots and physical therapy for my shoulder pain as needed. Some ointments were prescribed for my skin rash, but they did not help. I tried different salves, but nothing worked until I put athlete's foot cream on it. Holy smokes did that stuff burn when I put it on my legs, but the rash disappeared. Thank you, Lord!

A lot happened to me in those two years. One of the first things I did when I got home was to go to Birmingham with my sister Mavis and buy a brand-new Volkswagen car. I paid cash for it but had to have her sign with me because I would not turn twenty-one for a couple of months. Go figure! I could join the Marines, fight for my nation and get wounded, but I could not pay cash for my own car without someone twenty-one years of age or older signing the paper work with me. Welcome home, Jimmy!

Another little welcome home moment was when I went to the "Jack's Hamburgers" restaurant in the nearby town of Alabaster, Alabama and quaffed a beer in public with one of my high school friends, Lane Bristow. That was the wrong thing to do in a dry county! An overzealous Alabaster policeman ignoring all the others drinking in the restaurant parking area, arrested me for drinking a beer in public and charged me with supplying beer to underage drinkers. When you think about it, how could there be such a thing as underage drinkers in a dry county or how could alcoholic beverages be bought with ease all over a dry county? Ha! I tried to tell the policeman that I had just been discharged from the Marines a couple of days back and had totally forgotten that Shelby County, Alabama was a dry county. The policeman was basically calling me a bootlegger. Amazing! Thank goodness a couple of city council members remembered me from my high school days. The owner of the local "Western Auto" vouched for my good character and said that I had paid my bill in a timely manner. He also pointed out that no outstanding warrants were pending against me, probably because I had just been discharged from the Marines. After listening to what had happened at Jack's Hamburgers, I was admonished for drinking in public and all charges against me were dropped. Thank you for your patience, Lord! It appeared that I still had some stupid in me to eliminate.

Not long after the public drinking incident happened, my cousin, Bob Cain wanted to drive my new car. He wanted us to go to Montevallo, Alabama and talk to some girls he knew that were students at the University of Montevallo. While on the way to Montevallo, we passed the Methodist church in Siluria, Alabama and I saw a beautiful girl walking towards the church. She looked familiar and when we got close to her, I realized she had been a sophomore at my high school when I was a senior. Her name was Kathy Gowin. I told Bobby to turn around and drive up close to her where I could talk to her. He did and my life changed forever. I fell in love with her right then and there. Some say that is not possible. All I can say is too bad for them. The Lord totally turned my world right side up or upside down, however you want to look at it, when he placed Kathy in my life. I quickly learned what real love for the woman you would spend the rest of your life with was all about. Thank you, Lord!

I started going to classes at the University of Montevallo about three months after I was discharged from the Marines. I was blessed again by the Lord when he placed outstanding professors and advisors in my path. There were several of my professors that had suffered the effects of war in their lives. My major professor was Dr. E. B. Sledge. He was a World War Two Era Marine. Dr Sledge wrote a book about his war time experiences in the Pacific and another book about his extended duty in China after the war. Once again, I was blessed when I found out that because of my Purple Hearts and disability rating, the State of Alabama would pay for my tuition, books, supplies and provide a monthly stipend to help cover my living expenses. The State of Alabama also paid for Kathy's Master of Arts in Education degree and our children's college tuitions. I really appreciate my State providing me and my family with this honor. I graduated from the University of Montevallo in December, 1973 with a Bachelor of Science degree.

About two years into my college education, I started to have serious leg pains. It hurt so bad that I told Kathy that I wish they would just cut the leg off. That was pretty extreme thinking, but it was driving me crazy. My problems with my leg came to a head during a trip to my mom's house to visit with my aunt Judy. Aunt Judy was spending some time with mom before continuing her journey to Albuquerque, New Mexico. On the drive over to mom's house, the right front tire assembly started shaking the front end of our car so bad that I could barely steer the car. I had slid off an icy road near Springfield, Missouri and damaged the passenger side front tire assembly and tie rod while driving back to Alabama from a Christmas vacation in Commerce, Oklahoma, where Kathy's family lived. I thought I had fixed the problem, but something was not right with the tire assembly or the tie rod. When the tire assembly and tie rod caused trouble, I could feel vibrations in the steering wheel. When I felt the vibrations, I would pull the car over to the shoulder of the road, get out of the car and kick the tire a couple of times. Usually, that would take care of the problem. Go figure! This time when I kicked the tire, I felt and heard something "pop" in my left leg. The leg immediately went limp and I could not stand on it. I managed to get back in the car and Kathy drove us to my mom's house. The next day Kathy drove me to the V.A. hospital in Birmingham. My leg was not only limp but was now numb. Old Jimmy had really messed up this time. Dad gum Vietnam!

Have I mentioned how the Lord has blessed me before? Well, he now provided me with another gigantic blessing in the form of the chief orthopedic surgeon that taught orthopedic surgery at the University of Alabama's Medical

School campus in Birmingham, Alabama. The x-ray technicians had taken x-rays of my leg, but the orthopedic doctor on duty at the time was having trouble figuring out what was wrong with my leg. The chief orthopedic surgeon overheard the conversation about my leg and walked over and introduced himself to me. He basically took over at that time and ordered more x-rays, personally overseeing my case. He was very persistent and after several more x-rays, figured out what was wrong with my leg. He told me that I had shrapnel in my knee that was obstructing the nerves passing through the knee causing trauma to my leg that could possibly lead to an amputation if not treated. He recommended that I immediately have an operation to remove the shrapnel and repair the damage. I told him I was in the process of signing up for my next semester's classes and I needed to be there to ensure I got the classes needed to graduate. He said that I could go and do that, but he would probably have to amputate my leg when I came back to the V.A. hospital. He told me that it was my call. I asked him where I could buy a toothbrush. They operated on my leg the next morning. When they removed the shrapnel, it felt like someone had removed a ten-ton weight off my leg. I let out an audible sigh that got the doctors and nurses laughing. My doctor asked me if I had felt anything and I told him no, but my leg sure did feel better. That really cracked all of them up. It took six or seven months for my leg to completely heal and to get back to my normal routine. I have not had any more trouble with severe pain in my leg since that operation. Thank you, Lord!

It turned out that I did not have to worry about the classes I needed for my next semester of college. Dr. Sledge arranged for me to be signed up in every class I needed. He even had the college book store set aside what books and materials I would need. Dr. Sledge was featured in the "Band of Brothers - The Pacific" HBO mini-series. He was a great Marine, a great professor and a fine gentleman. I will always remember our talks about life in the Marines, combat, bird watching, field trips and the Biology classes I signed up for because he was the instructor. He was a tough professor but fair. He not only taught me a lot about Science in general and Biology in particular, but he also taught me a lot about life.

16

P.T.S.D. and C.L.L.

Several years ago, when we had troops in Somalia, U.S. Army soldiers were ambushed and took several casualties in Mogadishu. One evening after work, I happened to see the news coverage of an Army soldier being dragged through the streets of Mogadishu. People were kicking him, beating his body with sticks and slicing him with machetes. Something snapped in my mind and I started screaming and cussing at the television. I could not believe a national news outlet would show someone's son being treated like that. Shame on them! I literally wanted to go to the news station and burn it down to the ground. Something happened that I could not explain to anyone that night. My Vietnam had come back to haunt me nearly thirty years after I had been there. I now know it was called P.T.S.D. or Post Traumatic Stress Disorder. P.T.S.D. started affecting my mind and my actions immediately after the screaming at the television episode and gradually got worse. There were many little signs. My behavior deteriorated. I seemed to focus my anger at my oldest son, the most. Forgive me Jamie. I would lose track of time and forget what I was doing. I caught myself thinking about my Vietnam experience more and more.

Two things brought my problems to the point where I realized I needed help. Have you ever seen fear in your wife's and your son's eyes? I did and it shamed me. The next thing that happened to convince me that I needed some help was when I missed my Interstate 20/59 Brookwood, Alabama turn-off and ended up on the shoulder of the Interstate in Meridian, Mississippi across from the airport and the Air National Guard base. I did not have a clue how or when I had gotten there. The deep "Wop - Wop - Wop" sound of CH-47 or UH-1 helicopters landing and taking off at the nearby National Guard Airbase triggered a thought that I was back in Vietnam. I thought I needed to hurry up and get loaded for a search and destroy mission. For a few seconds I could not square away in my mind the relationship between the vehicle traffic racing by me on the interstate along with the helicopters landing and taking off nearby or why I was sitting in the vehicle I was sitting in. I was thinking that the air conditioning sure does feel good and then I was asking myself what air conditioning? I guess the sheer craziness in my mind about what was going on around me finally snapped me back to the reality of where I was, and the moment of time I was in. The whole experience was a real conundrum to me. The next day I went to the Tuscaloosa, Alabama V.A. hospital and fortunately was able to talk to a psychologist.

Once again, the Lord stepped in and blessed me. There was a P.T.S.D. out-patient program at the V.A. hospital in Tuscaloosa. The two men that mentored the participants of the P.T.S.D. group I was in were extraordinary individuals. Both were psychologists. One of them had been a med-evac helicopter pilot in Vietnam and the other was a Methodist minister. They guided me through a three hour per day P.T.S.D. meeting, two days a week for eighteen months. Sometime during the seventeenth month, I started letting everything that had been bottled up in my mind since I was a boy come out in the open where I could deal with it. P.T.S.D. does not just affect combat veterans. It can affect anyone that has suffered abuse, been involved in accidents, tragedies or other life changing events. I did not realize that part of my P.T.S.D. problem was a byproduct of my alcoholic Dad and his abuse toward his family. When I started dealing with all the things I had bottled up in my mind over the years, I was able to confront each issue separately and deal with it. Believe me, it is not an easy endeavor. Also, I had a better understanding of why I suffered the "Survivor's Guilt" that plagued me. It was a symptom of the P.T.S.D. I was suffering from.

One of my mentors made a profound statement about the wonder of the mind and a P.T.S.D. moment. He said the mind is like a giant video recorder that can store and catalog everything that is going on around you. The sights, sounds, colors, smells, texture of things touched, action or movement, both subtle and obvious, even your intuitive feel of things are interconnected in the mind. The mind stores all this information, using only what is needed at the moment, storing the rest for use when needed. When you least expect it, a sound, smell, noise or something seen can trigger this storage area in such a way that everything floods the mind at once causing a good or a bad reaction that overwhelms the mind's ability to deal rationally with what is happening

Page 109

around you. That is a P.T.S.D. moment. The best way to deal with it is to confront it and own it. Sounds pretty simple, right? Wrong! For some it is simple, but for others it can be a miserable experience, even leading to suicide.

Because of the excellent counseling and mentoring I received at the V.A. hospital in Tuscaloosa, I was able to overcome my P.T.S.D. problem and move on with my life. I had never really talked about my Vietnam experiences with my family and I was finally able to open up to them a bit. Some things you need to confront, turn them over to the Lord and walk away from them. I realized I could not be what I wanted to be to my family until I sought help for myself to confront my P.T.S.D. related issues. Once I did this, I was able to share my thoughts and concerns with them. They witnessed the angry, irrational side effects of P.T.S.D. working within me. As they watched me continuously learning about and overcoming my P.T.S.D. issues, they were able to not fear me. I needed to show them I was working hard to get control because my family is one of the most precious things in my life and I did not want to lose them. As I have said many times, the Lord has continuously interceded in my life with his mercy and grace. He continues to bless me and my family over and over. Thank you, Lord!

In 2004, I was diagnosed with C.L.L. or Chronic Lymphocytic Leukemia brought about from possible exposure to Agent Orange, a herbicide used to defoliate plants and trees in Vietnam thereby exposing enemy positions. I was told that I would not live past my sixty-fifth birthday. Talk about a head on encounter with mortality! Kathy and I immediately turned to the Lord in prayer. I have to admit that at first, I could not lay it down and let the Lord intercede on my behalf. Eventually, I did. Some may not believe in the power of prayer, but I do. A group of my Christian friends placed their hands on me and lifted me up in prayer. It was a very powerful moment and I experienced a tingling sensation throughout my body. Some may scoff, but at my next appointment with my oncologist, I was informed that my blood analysis had stabilized. Since the initial estimate of my demise, my oncologist has changed his original prognosis of my life expectancy because of my stabilized blood analysis. I have been advised that I might have a lot of years left past sixty-five. I am now sixty-nine and remain in what is called the "zero" stage of my leukemia. I have to get infusions on a regular basis to help my body fight off infections and I have been very careful not to get around anyone that is sick. At least the initial fear or trepidation I felt when

I learned about my cancer is gone. Once again, the Lord interceded in my life with his mercy and grace. Thank you, Lord!

17

Reflections

All of us have experienced catastrophes that have in some way affected us. In my little community of Simmsville, Alabama, there were at least four of us that served in Vietnam. Several of us were wounded. Most of our families had telephones that were on a "party line" system. Sometimes, when someone saw a military vehicle on Shelby County Highway 11, the main road through our community, they would call ahead and alert anyone they could about the military vehicle. When I was wounded, the Marines notified my mom by telegram and followed the telegram up with a visit from a Marine notification team out of Bessemer, Alabama. The first two times they notified mom at the farm, she bravely met them at the front door. When the notification team walked up to the front door the third time to notify mom that I had been med-evaced to the Naval Hospital in Agana, Guam, she ran out the back door. She must have seen or heard about them coming and thought that this time the news would not be good. The notification team quickly understood what was going on and ran around to the back of the house shouting: "He is okay Mrs. Kitson, he is okay." Just thinking of what my mom, my family and all of the families had to go through, breaks my heart. To think that some were notified of their loved one's death on a battle field half a world away is unimaginable. A son or daughter's time in the service, especially while our nation is at war, can be a gigantic emotional roller coaster for everyone involved. I think our armed services are trying to address this stress issue better. Even so, military, veterans and their families are being adversely affected by multiple deployments and system overloads in government services.

Unfortunately, you just cannot erase some terrible images completely from your mind. My beautiful wife, Kathy, has been awakened many times during our marriage by my thrashing and yelling brought on by a nightmare of something from my Vietnam experience. Thankfully, the counseling I received at the V.A. helped me deal with not only the bad dreams and nightmares associated with my Vietnam experience, but also with issues I had repressed from my childhood days concerning my dad's alcohol abuse. I have had less problems as the years have gone by and I give all of the credit for that to the Lord. I thank the Lord every day for allowing me to survive my Vietnam experience, to come back home to my family and for blessing me with my wife, children, grandchildren, family and friends.

Kathy and I have been married for forty-eight years, have two outstanding sons, a wonderful daughter-in-law and five beautiful grandchildren. I have been really blessed by the Lord with all of my family and Kathy's family. My mom died at age ninety-two. She was a real jewel. Kathy's dad and mom died several years ago. Her dad and I had a lot of fun fishing and golfing together. Her mom traveled with us on nearly all of our out-of-town trips. Kathy's dad and mom were outstanding individuals. Kathy's sister, Rea Kelley, is now a regular travel companion on our out of town trips like their mom was. We have had a lot of fun traveling to different places around the country, even overseas. My sisters, brother, family and friends have all been instrumental in providing me with a loving, patient and understanding environment, enabling me to deal with the "Vietnam Moments" that occasionally trouble me.

Unlike some Vietnam veterans, I have been blessed with a productive life with much happiness and many pleasant memories. I retired about ten years ago. For over thirty-five years I helped remove the scars left behind by surface and underground coal mining activities. I was able to restore coal mined lands to as close to their original, pre-mine condition as possible. The ability to repair the damage caused by coal mining operations and watch ecosystems regenerate led to a very satisfying career. I suppose that you could call my coal mine reclamation career the antithesis to the death and destruction I witnessed in Vietnam. Unfortunately, there are many veterans that have not found happiness, nor have they been able to deal positively with their physical wounds and P.T.S.D. nightmares, causing them to suffer failed family relationships, drug abuse, alcoholism, homelessness and even suicide. We need to be aware of their conditions and show them empathy by trying our best to help them when and where we can. There are many organizations trying to help but if an individual does not want help, you cannot help them.

A person must want to seek help and work at it to succeed. Believe me when I say that it is not an easy thing to do!

Some did not make it back home alive, leaving a void in the lives of their family members. I did not know about the death of one of my childhood friends until I was discharged. His name was Sammy Copeland. We were the best of friends when I lived in my grandfather's house in Birmingham, Alabama. We went to school together, played baseball together and often spent the night at each other's house. Sammy had joined the Marines and was sent to Vietnam about a year after me. I saw his name along with the names of my squad members on the "Vietnam Memorial Wall" when I went to Washington, D.C. on a business trip a few years back. While I was looking at his name etched on the wall, I said a prayer for him and his family. I could even picture us riding our bikes and playing baseball in my mind. I placed a piece of paper over his name that was etched into the wall and rubbed a pencil back and forth over his name until his name was transcribed onto the paper. I told him "Semper Fi, Sammy." Rest in peace.

Several of the people I have mentioned have been able to get on with their lives, putting their wounds and combat experiences behind them. Some have not. Others have struggled, but for the most part been able to lead productive, happy lives. Paul Reynolds and his wife live in South Georgia. I have heard Paul reminisce about Vietnam. Paul has a great faith in the Lord and has been able to lead a productive life outside the Marines. We exchange Christmas cards. The last I heard about Jim Bembry was that he was a deputy sheriff somewhere in Texas. I hope he has had a successful career and a happy life. Wayne Thornton married his high school sweetheart and raised their children in North Carolina. I have been able to talk to him and his wife on the phone and we have sent letters or cards to each other occasionally. Wayne has struggled with his wounds and P.T.S.D. symptoms since his discharge from the Marines. Alton Srygley lives near Harpersville, Alabama. He has struggled with P.T.S.D. symptoms for years. His Vietnam experience haunts him practically every day. He was a machine gunner and machine gun section leader in the Fifth Marines during the 1968 Tet New Year battle for Hue. Terry Kuntsler died in 2002. I have not seen nor heard anything about Lawrence P. Nodine (Nody) since I left Camp Lejeune. When Dr. E. B. Sledge came home from the Pacific and his China duty after World War Two, he eventually found his niche as a college professor teaching Biology at the

Page 114

University of Montevallo. He had a successful career and a happy life with his beautiful wife and two sons. Dr. Sledge had his P.T.S.D. moments when he came home. I think his books "With the Old Breed" and "China Marine" not only established him as a well-known writer but served as a catharsis from his combat experiences. Dr. Sledge died a few years ago. It was an honor to serve as a pallbearer at his funeral service in Montevallo, Alabama. The United States Marine Corps honored him at his burial service in Mobile, Alabama. Ronald Thompson died in the horrific ambush I mentioned on page 62 in chapter eight, "Combat Patrol." Six more of our squad died that day plus several were wounded. I was not there with them that terrible day because I was in the hospital recovering from wounds received from a booby trap explosion. As I have said, the Lord works in mysterious ways. Thank, you Lord! Now you know my story, the story of Jimmy, the Marine. Watch out for what you wish for!

I have included a couple of poems and some pictures that might make what I have written about a little bit more interesting. My youngest son, Jake, is a Lieutenant Colonel in the United States Army. He is an Orthodontist with Paratrooper wings, a Pathfinder badge, an Air Assault badge, a Field Medic badge and other ribbons denoting his career in the Army. I have included two of Jake's poems he honored me and other veterans with. My wife Kathy wrote "Reflections of a Vietnam Veteran" after I returned from a business trip in Washington D. C. I explained to her that the "Vietnam Memorial Wall" had really affected me deeper than I thought it would. I told her that I walked the length of the black, highly polished Gabbro wall, then walked far enough away from it that I could see the entire wall at once. When I tried to remember the specific names I was looking for, I could not. Up close the names were a blur because of my tears. A park ranger asked if he could be of assistance to me. He showed me how to look up names by name or date, but I just could not remember any names. I told him I was having a hard time trying to get control of my emotions. He told me that he understood and that the reason he worked there at the "Vietnam Memorial Wall" was because his son's name was on it. Wow! I finally remembered my childhood friend's name and some of the names of my squad members. I took the pencil and paper that the ranger gave to me and transcribed each name onto the paper by placing the paper against the name and rubbing the pencil lead over each name. I still get emotional when I think about that trip to the "Vietnam Memorial Wall." "Semper Fi, Marines!" Rest in peace.

MEMORIAL SERVICE
2ND BATTALION, 3RD MARINES
3 February 1968
****

Let all who gather here do so in silent remem-
brance of those who made the supreme sacrifice.

ASSEMBLE THE BATTALION

INVOCATION AND LORD'S PRAYER..........CHAPLAIN

HYMN....."FAITH OF OUR FATHERS".....CONGREGATION

SCRIPTURE AND MEDITATION..............CHAPLAIN

MEMORIAL REMARKS...............LTCOL J. W. DAVIS

ROLL CALL OF THE DEPARTED...SGTMAJ R. W. MILLER

"TAPS"......................SGT G. H. BRUN

HYMN......."ETERNAL FATHER".......CONGREGATION

Eternal Father, Strong to save,
Whose arm hath bound the restless wave,
Who biddest the mighty ocean deep
It's own appointed limits keep;
O hear us when we cry to thee
For those in peril on the sea.

Eternal Father, grant, we pray,
To all Marines, both night and day,
The courage, honor, strength, and skill,
Their land to serve, Thy law fulfill;
Be thou the Shield forevermore
From ev'ry peril to the Corps.

BENEDICTION...........................CHAPLAIN

IN MEMORY

GOLF COMPANY

CAPT ROESLER, JOHN O.
2 LT RAMSTEAD, JAMES T.
LCPL BENNETT, CLIFFORD R.
PFC BISJAK, HOWARD R.
PFC DRAKE, RICHARD K. JR.
PFC ODOM, STEVEN C.
PFC PITNER, MONTE G.
PFC POWERS, WILLIAM J.
PFC TATE, CHARLES T. JR.
PFC THOMPSON, RONALD E.

ECHO COMPANY

PFC HOLMES, CLEVELAND
PFC CHRYSTYNYCZ, THEODORE

FOX COMPANY

PFC LEOS, NARCISO JR.

HOTEL COMPANY

LCPL HANDLEY, CRAIG W.
PFC CARPENTER, GARY R.
PFC EVANS, ALBERT
PFC SINGLETON, ARTHUR D.
PFC SPILKER, KENNETH A.

"For we know that if the earthly house of our
tabernacle be dissolved, we have a building
from God, a house not made with hands, eternal,
in the heavens."

2 Corinthians 5:1

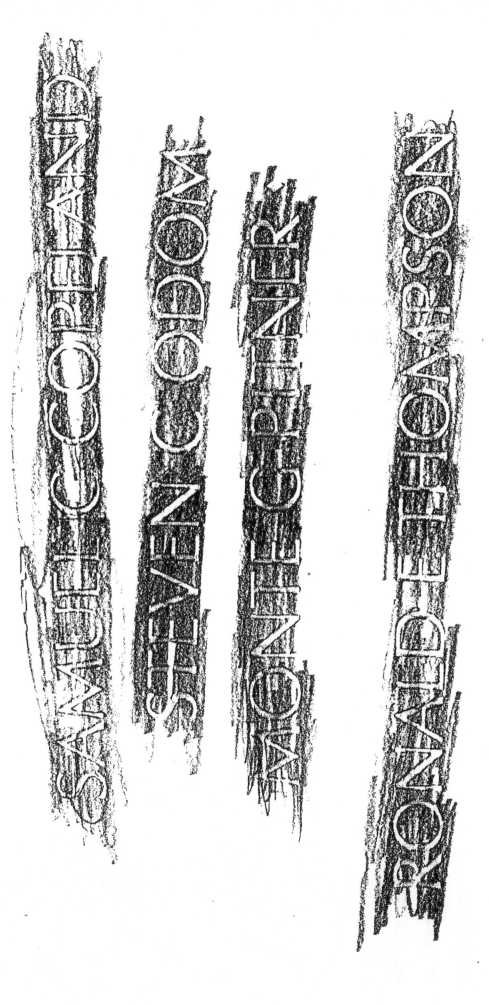

SAMUEL COPELAND

STEVEN CODRON

MONTE GRINER

RONALD THOMPSON

"The Marine"

By Jim Kitson

I will always be a Marine.
Parris Island molded me.
I was not a hero.
I was a "grunt."
I did my duty; said "Aye Aye Sir"
Walked point, tail-end Charlie, and in between.
Firefights fought, wounds suffered, and horrific sights seen.
Bonded forever with fellow Marines.
Combat tempered our souls.
I will not forget.
Many, like me, will never forget.

"The Patrol"

By Jim Kitson

Put your boots on boys, it's time for a walk.
Sarge says: "Silence your gear and keep down the talk."
As we part the wire, danger is near.
We hope our trembling doesn't betray our fear.
Mom and Dad can't help us, we're on our own.
Trust your buddy, your training, and the strength of home.

One last look, our perimeter is no more.
One quick prayer, "Lord spare us the gore."
Beware, the trail, we've been here before.
Booby traps, ambushes, snipers are lore.
We quit worrying long ago how we would fare.
We quit worrying of ordinary things, for death is in the air.

Our jackets, helmets, webbing and gear,
Do little to help ease our aching fear.
We've loaded our pockets with supplies of death.
The grenades, ammunition, mortar round and L.A.W. suck at our breath.
Our rifles are cradled with instinctive loving care.
Our friends support us with the help of the air.

When rifles are firing and machine guns speak.
We know not the time, not even the week.
The roar of artillery, the screech of the F-4,
The rattle of the chopper, the tank not noticed before.
It's survival that matters, no time to think.
We've gone on automatic, it's our military link.

We cringe from the vibrations, the noise is beyond belief,
Wounded, killed, alive, the end is relief.
When the firing is done and we've survived again,
We stare at the bodies amongst them our friends.
The officers say we've done very well.
There's water, "C" rations, re-supply and mail.

This patrol is turning home, just a few more miles.
As we near the perimeter there are no smiles.
Has the recognition pattern been changed when we pop our flares?
This is when fear is real, you see it in our stares.
We cross through the wire, bunkers on left and right.
We've survived again, but how many are left to fight?

The wounds add up, death is cheated here and there.
Some of us are med-evaced, relief is in the air.
Hospitals and duty stations are part of the rest.
Some of us have made it, we are part of the best.
The silence of the ground has enveloped so many brave men.
A monument we stare at, the tears never end.

"Freedom Returns In The Silence Of Night"

By Jim Kitson

The silence of night, false protection lulls us.
Sound deadening darkness engulfs us with noise.
Alertness of the watch numbs our feelings.
The unknown runs rampart in our mind.
Senses betrayed, reality of war.
Animal instinct, acting without thought.
Scream of survival, adrenalin to our body.
Soul betrayed, question of courage.

Light, the brightness blinds us.
Noise, a choreographed death unfolds.
Keys to life are vigilance and reaction.
Darkness, we see again.

Dreams, stupor we must sort it out.
Life moves onward, we have survived.
Passing of time invigorates our soul.
New life to build, families grow.

Horrors of dreams, the past returns.
Fall of survival, minds unraveled.
Dreams, reality, life moves forward.
The compassion of man nurtures the soul.

Silence of the night, trust of those fallen.
Memories cataloged dreams put aside.
Fears, dreams, a mind runs rampart no more.
Family and friends, a life returns.

"Reflections of a Vietnam Veteran"

By Kathy Kitson

He boarded a plane to Washington, D. C. on business. He wanted to see the Vietnam Memorial.

His hotel was within walking distance. The black, shiny granite blended

into the landscape. The walls reflected trees, lawns and people looking for a name.

Fifty-eight thousand, three hundred and eighteen names. He stands unable to move. Tears blur his vision.

Bullets snap past his head, he turns and sees a buddy dead. Steps in hole lined with grenades and almost loses his leg.

Blown from a tank and wiping blood from his head. Staring at a dead V. C. laying across his legs.

Crawling with a dislocated shoulder away from the V. C. in the tree line. Firing at an imaginary figure of Christ. Talking to a Priest who helps him sleep at night.

Writing letters to mothers about their dead sons. Being called to set up ambushes and lead a patrol. He did not have to be there, could have stayed in the rear because of his wounds.

Having his knee lock up, unable to run. Thinking of wounds and the hospital on Guam. Nearly drinking himself to death.

Unable to recall the dead from his platoon as he faces the wall.

Names come back as he boards the plane.

Note: The black, shiny granite is actually Gabbro, which is sometimes called black granite. When I was looking for an up-to-date number of names (as of 2017) on the Memorial, I noticed that the stone used to construct the Memorial was Gabbro. I always thought it was black granite.

"A New Generation"

By Jake Kitson
05/01/05

A new generation ponders
How do I say thanks to those in their graves
Or to those who still walk with war's heavy weight
I see great monuments and living monuments all over the place
Heroes who never wanted to be
A new generation left to rest and wrestle with the things
That simply can't be explained

A new generation re-lives an old Marine's tears
Scarred with horror, marked with honor
One went down, you moved on
Life has stopped and life has gone on
Sacrifices unseen, done
A new generation left to rest and wrestle with the things
That simply can't be explained

A new generation learns of an old Marine's tears
A father tells a son
How life has stopped and life has gone on
About sacrifices unseen, done
So a new generation has the freedom to go on
While an old generation rests and wrestles with the things
That simply can't be explained

A new generation re-lives an old Marine's tears
This was the only thing the old generation feared
Scarred with horror, marked with honor
One goes down' one moves on
Life has stopped and life has gone on
Sacrifices unseen, done
A new generation left to wrestle with the things
That simply can't be explained

A new generation re-lives an old Marine's tears
A desert in a far off place
As names are called with no response
Solemn silence
Kevlar helmets on rifle butts stand
And a new generation tears stain the sand
They are left to rest and wrestle with the things
That simply can't be explained

A new generation will ponder and give thanks

"Welcome Home"

A soldier in a terminal
With a smile on his face
Waiting for home, thinking about today
Only two short weeks
He'll be back in that place
Walking to his greeting, he can hardly wait
A hug, a kiss, I love you son
Lest we forget, welcome home

A plane full of soldiers
Flags honor their beds
These have come home
Moms and Dads weep over their dead
Full measure of devotion each has shown
Another folded flag passed on
Lest we forget, welcome home

It doesn't matter the war
No man left behind
This value is core
The jungles of Vietnam
Or a desert in Iraq
We're all going in
And we're all coming back
A tomb with unknown members
Guarded from dawn till dawn
Lest we forget, welcome home

Jake Kitson
Memorial Day, 2003

Made in the USA
Columbia, SC
26 May 2019